The Competitive Edge

The Eight Efficiency Factors
For Continuous Improvement

MANAGEMENT

BOUNDARIES

HUMAN
RESOURSES

MATERIALS

MANUFACTURING
COSTS

EQUIPMENT

CONTINUOUS
IMPROVEMENTS

NON-VALUE
ADDED COSTS

ENVIRONMENT

ADVANCING
TECHNOLOGY

OUTSOURCING

TARGETS

MEASURES

QUALITY • CUSTOMER SATISFACTION

by
Joseph McHugh

Published by AuthorHouse 03/18/2017

ISBN: 978-1-4184-0128-3 (sc)

Library of Congress Control Number: 2004091440

Print information available on the last page.

This book is printed on acid free paper.

THE COMPETITIVE EDGE
CONTINUOUS IMPROVEMENTS FOR BUSINESS, EDUCATION, AND GOVERNMENT

Those who govern, having much business on their hands, do not generally like to take the trouble of considering and carrying into execution new projects. The best public measures are, therefore, seldom adopted from previous wisdom, but are forced by the occasion.
Benjamin Franklin 1794

How easy it is to earn a living today, on yesterday's knowledge, but how often it leads to obsolescence.
Frederick Hertzburg

Traditional Mode of Thinking

Things are as they have always been—therefore they could not be any other way.

The Critical Mode of Thinking:

Everything is to be considered possible, unless it is proven to be impossible.
George Soros

To work without meaning is wasteful.
To work with meaning provides for pride, satisfaction, and success.
Joseph McHugh

A Guiding Principle

Change...
so essential to success.
Joseph McHugh

Acknowledgments

The contents herein were made possible by the many people I have been fortunate enough to meet during my career, be they positive or negative relationships, because in some way they have influenced my thinking and business strategies.

To my wife Betty, whom I married when there were 220,000,000 people in America. I picked the best of the best, and by so doing, I won the greatest lottery of all.

To my children, Karen, Linda, Donna, and Joseph, who continue to bring recognition to the family because of their commitment to the best moral and ethical standards of our society.

To Nancy Middlemas, who assigned me "homework" to keep my creative thinking on track. She provided the editing and layout talent so necessary to complete this continuous improvement plan.

Table of Contents

Efficiency Factor #1 HUMAN RESOURCES..2

Efficiency Factor #2 MATERIALS 10

Efficiency Factor #3 EQUIPMENT 17

Efficiency Factor #4 ENVIRONMENT..25

Efficiency Factor #5 OUTSOURCING 30

Efficiency Factor #6 ADVANCING TECHNOLOGIES 38

Efficiency Factor #7 NON-VALUE-ADDED COSTS 42

Efficiency Factor #8 MANUFACTURING COSTS............................51

Measurements of Management X-MATRIX 59

Do It Now! THE PLAN 62

Preface

Following the Industrial Revolution, American enterprise reaped financial benefits forged by that period's industrial leaders. America became a benchmark for the world, with increasing technology, productivity, work ethics, and an overall commitment to excellence. But as time passed, we fell victim to the rewards of our mounting affluence. As the quality of our goods and services slipped, we were faced with foreign competition, and for the first time, America struggled to maintain world leadership.

As our competitive edge began to slip away, leaders in business, education, and government simply passed on inefficient costs to willing customers. In a climate of limited financial planning, the motto became "Spend for today, because tomorrow will be even better." This narrow vision has placed undue hardships on today's management and work force, because it failed to recognize the challenges of a global economy.

Now, two decades past the high-flying '80s, most American institutions are realizing that our period of prosperity has succumbed to an era of conservative spending forced on us by global competition. World economies, especially those of emerging nations, have challenged U.S. companies into rekindling their competitive drive. Consequently, management people are struggling to find avenues for improvement.

> *Competitiveness of the Global Economy*

And now the speed of these adjustments becomes the key to maintaining and recapturing market share coupled with profitability. It's a safe bet that success in the future will require *The Competitive Edge*.

Unfortunately, American institutions have fallen prey to serious inefficiencies, as evidenced by lowered educational achievement, governmental gridlock, plant shutdowns, downsizing, mergers, and foreign takeovers. Today, in all corners of the nation, American management is seeking unique individuals who possess drive, determination, and commitment to improving productivity in all areas.

Management will no longer accept the inefficiencies of the past, nor the passiveness of the present, but will be more demanding of the future.

Productivity is a given, a must, a foundation for continuous improvements because **productivity is the universal avenue to success**. The key to this success is the level of management's commitment. We must rekindle the energy and conceptual skills each of us possesses and move forward to challenge global competition. We either stay the course or lead the charge for continuous improvements. And I might add, the caveat, **tomorrow is today.** Consequently, *The Competitive Edge* offers the dynamic program, *Do It Now!*

By offering sound managerial concepts to quicken the pace of transformation, it is my hope that this book will encourage change and move organizations towards continuous improvements and greater competitiveness. *The Competitive Edge* provides a plan consisting of Eight Efficiency Factors for turning inefficiencies into the necessary day-to-day productivity essential to success within an ever-expanding global economy: HUMAN RESOURCES, MATERIALS, EQUIPMENT, ENVIRONMENT, OUTSOURCING, ADVANCING TECHNOLOGIES, NON-VALUE-ADDED COSTS, AND MANUFACTURING COSTS.

You may be thinking, what about Quality and Customer Satisfaction? Those two terms are intentionally omitted because in today's competitive climate, they are a given. Any organization not founded on these fundamental values is not ready to apply the Eight Efficiency Factors.

The Eight Efficiency Factors, as defined here, are essential for the continuing success of any organization. Furthermore, all Eight Factors interrelate with each other, and consequently compound the **continuous improvements** and profitability. Due to their interrelationships, the Efficiency Factors offer a road map of opportunities to guide continuous improvements along

> Continuous
> improvements

numerous avenues. More importantly, an improvement in any one factor will, in most cases, create a positive effect on one or several other factors. For example, implementing the guidelines for the ENVIRONMENT Efficiency Factor, can simultaneously have a positive effect on MATERIALS and EQUIPMENT. As suggested throughout this book, when areas targeted for improvement are identified and implemented, other areas are positively impacted, thereby providing opportunities not previously anticipated. Remarkably, improvements in any *one* of the Eight Factors offers rapid benefits for the organization as a whole.

I believe that the immediate financial returns offered by the ideas in *The Competitive Edge* are so great, one would have to question why these proposed changes are not being implemented at a faster rate. The contents and outline of this book are designed for expediency, offering choices about which Efficiency Factor is in line with your most pressing need for improvements. I therefore trust the

Eight Efficiency Factors, as presented, are accessible enough for your immediate implementation.

Good luck on your never-ending journey for continuous improvements. ***Do it now!***

Introduction

Moving from Management 101 to Management 2001

Webster defines the term *management* as "the art of managing with a degree of skill." This definition suggests that management practices remain something of an art form rather than a science. But does this hold true? Have we not, over the past two hundred years, learned more about managing businesses with worldwide interests? One would certainly think so. Is the art of managing a business simply a continuation of Management 101, as implied by the trite saying, "Let's get back to basics"?

Today Rockwell International suggests that the purpose of management is "To lead, to guide, to capitalize on the present, while providing for the future." This definition, in my professional judgment, embodies the managerial commitment essential for tomorrow's success. Consequently, as we begin our journey through *The Competitive Edge* this will be the underlying theme of this stimulating campaign toward cost-effectiveness and its ultimate reward: higher profits.

This management journey will focus on Eight Efficiency Factors:

The Eight Efficiency Factors	
Human Resources	Materials
Equipment	Environment
Outsourcing	Advancing Technologies
Non-Value-Added Costs	Manufacturing Costs

Our first task is to review the basic management requirements of those individuals who have taken up the charter of managing business, education, and government entities in a global economy. The expanding global village of the new millennium will continue to exert leadership pressures far beyond the demands limited by our shorelines.

During the '70s and '80s I had the pleasant opportunity to work and implement these Eight Efficiency Factors in Italy and Poland. To be successful, I initially had to focus on the cultures of the work force in each new country. Almost immediately I realized that my American style of management had to be adjusted because of the new diversity I was exposed to.

During my Italian assignment, I was chartered to assist a new management team in implementing the management practices and operating policies of an American parent company. I was successful in doing so only after adjusting many practices and policies to collectively support the managerial thinking of both countries.

One vivid example of managerial adjustment involved the level of product quality accepted by the Italian management versus the American product quality level. The Italian standard for quality, as is true in many other parts of the world, is more difficult to achieve because consumers, unlike American consumers, are more quality-oriented rather than price-oriented. As a consequence, the intraplant reject levels in Italy exceed those of their counterparts in the U.S. This disparity created a great deal of misunderstanding between both managements until we adjusted.

Another area of considerable disagreement involved the managerial tone and approach to any given business challenge. For example, Italian managers spent considerable time debating an issue, while the American managerial style involved listening briefly to both sides, followed by an immediate course of action rendered by the top American manager. The operational tone in Italy appeared to be very emotional. I say "appeared to be," because Italians communicate daily with what seems to Americans as highly charged emotions, when in fact it is simply their way of communicating. Also, unlike American management teams who use first names in addressing each other, Italian management personnel, for the most part, do not know the first names of their colleagues. Therefore, I had to adjust my management style by addressing my peers by their family name without using *Mr.* or *Mrs.*

Then working in Eastern Europe required me to adapt to another kind of cultural diversity. In Poland during the '70s, socialists and governmental officials made all the major business decisions. My charter was to implement an extensive technology-transfer contract profitably. Here again I had to spend time learning the business culture of the Polish managers I was dealing with. Their managerial style differed because of the socialistic environment, i.e., local managers were reluctant to make decisions for fear of losing face with government authorities. As a consequence, all meetings had to be documented by written protocol. If a weighty matter were to be resolved, I would propose a solution and immediately my Polish counterparts would suggest that my solution be typed into the minutes of the meeting. My success overseas was due primarily to learning the cultures and diversity of the individuals with whom I was working.

At any rate, aside from the different management styles and diversity, I found both the Italians and Poles to be professionally committed to achieving the highest results for their management. The first challenge for American management is learning to deal professionally with diversity.

For years now, whether one is willing to accept it or not, America has evolved with many kinds of diversity within our borders. We have learned to accommodate the regional variances of those raised in all areas of this great land.

> *Culture and*
> *Diversity Training*

Management practices in the Northeast require a different set of skills than say, those in the Sun Belt or the Pacific Northwest. Consequently, the transfer of a manager from one corner of America to another requires a period of cultural adjustment.

For example, a manager leaving the fast-paced Northeast to work in the South must learn to tone down his or her managerial style. Couple this with the demands of working within a global economy, and one can readily anticipate a further expansion of managerial styles. Yet knowing this, many companies fail to provide proper cultural and diversity training for those who relocate or interact with people throughout the world. This, then, is one of many Management 2001 requirements to be addressed before implementing the Eight Efficiency Factors.

The next basic question a manager should ask is this: Who is managing America? Are those of us in management leading the charge or passively watching our ship teeter on the waves of inefficiency? Far too often managers sit back and rest on the successes of their predecessors. When it comes to inefficiency, misunderstandings frequently arise about who, for example, decides to shut down an inefficient unit. Strangely enough, sometimes local management and employees, lacking a plan for continuous improvements, actually close their own inefficient units, rather than top management.

For example, during the '80s, I was assigned to a Mid-western plant, chartered to "turn it around or we shut it down." Management had taken this position

> *Continuous*
> *Improvements*

because the company was losing money due to inefficiencies at the plant. Not knowing the technology, I nevertheless worked with the local management team and implemented an immediate cost-reduction program, conveying to higher management our excitement to improve the plant's performance immediately.

Following several months of the team's commitment, we slowly gained management approval and protected the well-being of some 1700 employees. As the months passed and we continued to demonstrate our continuous improvement efforts, we ultimately recaptured the support of the top management. In fact, the plant's life was extended for a period of ten years before being purchased by a foreign company. This is a vivid example of local management and employees virtually asking for a shut-down of an inefficient plant by failing to show top management visible, continuous improvements.

Consequently, business, education, and government entities must rise to the challenge of continuous improvements because competitive challenges from around the world will simply obliterate those with sub-standard performances. Management, from the supervision of few, to the heights of the executive committee, must be professionally demanding of everyone in the organization. Otherwise competition will continue to gain market share, seek innovative skills, and drain the cream of managerial talent. And let us not forget: **internationalism, with all its challenges, is here to stay.**

To meet the challenges of internationalism, we all must revitalize our drive, determination, and conceptual skills, for we have reached a level of affluence we no longer can afford. As managers, we must resist defining what we believe to be an individual's maximum productivity level and instead allow everyone the **freedom of professional expression.**

We must encourage change because **change is essential to success.** Today, if workers continue to perform their jobs the same way as yesterday, rest assured that the competition will soon outpace them. Passive or redundant positions and practices are a thing of the past.

Change...so essential to success

Management can no longer accept the inefficiencies of the past, nor the passiveness of the present, but must be more demanding of the future.

To accelerate efficiency, I offer the following *Do-It-Now* program. *"Do-It-Now"* means exactly as the phrase suggests. For example, if one has an idea for increasing efficiency, then simply *do it now* rather than calling a meeting where colleagues merely take notes, pay lip service, and never actually do anything to implement change. By granting **freedom of professional expression**, we gain an immediate competitive edge.

While assigned to a manufacturing unit in Southern California, I encouraged a management team to consider the removal of 90 feet of a power-driven conveyor by implementing the *Do-It-Now* concept. The team reviewed the possibility of the reduction at the assembly line. To my pleasant surprise, during the following weekend the conveyor was removed; materials were passed along on table tops; space, utilities, and maintenance costs were reduced; and get this: quality and productivity improved!

In later chapters you will find programs that spell out these concepts in detail. For now, let's touch on a few guidelines of effective management. First, we all know that management must set boundaries and targets followed by clear measures. But the boundaries should not be so definitive as to limit individuals to a finite area of responsibility. Numerous times in my career, I have encouraged

Do It Now!

employees to go beyond their preconceived boundaries. Not once have I had to suggest to employees that they overstepped their bounds. This by itself makes a strong statement, one worthy of management's consideration.

Targets must be far-reaching, yet reasonably attainable. For example, a 10 percent improvement is hardly notable; instead we should be looking for nothing less than 35 percent. When we offer targets, we should strive for improvements in everything we do, from issuance of purchase orders to shipment of final goods and services. Far too often, especially in manufacturing, management focuses on production improvements, while support groups fail to measure the cost of invoices, logistics, and so on. Electronic Data Interchange (EDI) provides a perfect example of an essential improvement that many organizations neglect. Today, the service industry has leapfrogged other businesses by approaching the cutting edge of EDI. Our paychecks are direct deposited. Our mortgage payment is deducted from our checking account, and we use credit cards freely at the gas pump. Why then is it so hard for organizations to implement EDI?

Within one organization, we implemented EDI to handle material purchases by electronically sending purchase orders, receipts, confirmation of the shipment, and invoices. Within the immediate future, your competitors will cease the issuance of purchase orders and simply send production schedules to strategic suppliers who will deliver the goods without prompts from the user. This method of purchasing materials is already operational in Asia. Kindly remember, if your procedures today are as yesterday, your competition is in the fast lane. **Do-It-Now! Set your targets and go for it!**

As leaders in your organization, you should set healthy targets for continuous improvements and establish measures to monitor progress once per quarter. The management tools needed for *The Competitive Edge* involve both old and new methods:

- **Integrated Manufacturing**
- **Push-Button Technology**
- **Manufacturing Friendly Products**
- **Value-Added Analysis**
- **Productivity Measures**
- **High Level Activities**
- **X-Matrix**
- **Eight Efficiency Factors**

Our journey towards doing business in the new millennium continues with a brief description of the first seven of these important managerial targets and measures. Then our expedition will focus in depth on chapters devoted to each of the Eight Efficiency Factors.

INTEGRATED MANUFACTURING

INTEGRATED MANUFACTURING should be your first target because of the many non-value-added costs associated with expensive manufacturing costs. Integrated manufacturing creates the capability to produce dissimilar products in tandem, on the same production line. Today many managers are stuck in the outmoded belief that only producing similar products and sizes is cost effective. Too often management teams, especially in the financial community, monitor capital investment (production equipment) expenditure, but fail to realize the extent of non-value-added costs associated with logistics: the handling and warehousing of finished products prior to shipment.

The key to successful profitability calls for an organization's financial community and top management to look at all expenses, both value-added and non-value-added costs. Management must not continue to evaluate the return-on-investment based simply on how many units justify the investment. More on this negative drain of company profits will be presented in later chapters of our journey toward competitiveness.

PUSH-BUTTON TECHNOLOGY

PUSH-BUTTON TECHNOLOGY is, quite frankly, urgently needed by the manufacturing community. This technology provides an opportunity for the production-line worker to change equipment parameters each time model changes occur, simply by pushing a button. Today most organizations, or for that matter, office personnel depend on technical support groups to make the necessary model changes and parameter settings, all of which increase non-value-added costs.

Although many businesses are slowly moving in the right direction, the pace is too gradual to meet the continuing challenges of a global economy. Why should dozens of line workers stand idle, waiting for technical personnel to change equipment for different parameter settings, office computer updates, and so on? Too often, we as management tend to limit an employee's true capabilities by refusing to become reliant on those who are willing to learn new techniques. Instead, we provide additional personnel who add no value to the product or service.

Furthermore, the initial design of a product or service should take into consideration the reduction of non-value-added costs. Therefore all design or re-design decisions should also be aimed towards *manufacturing friendly products and services.*

MANUFACTURING FRIENDLY PRODUCTS

MANUFACTURING FRIENDLY PRODUCTS reduces labor requirements so that companies and organizations will not have to search the world for inexpensive labor, but will be able to assemble products within the markets served. Can you imagine the positive financial impact and competitive edge a company might gain in this dynamic global economy? Moreover, the reduction of non-value-added costs (my greatest challenge to management) would be such a financial plus to any organization, I can't help but wonder why all managers have not redirected their efforts and answered the cost-effective call.

Manufacturing friendly products often requires only modest modifications. For example, the assembly of plastic components should not require nearly its current number of metal screws, because plastic has memory, meaning simply that squeezing the plastic into position and releasing it provides for the fastening desired. Unfortunately, far too many designers and managers take a passive position, quivering, "We better not." But the competitive global economy demands that we take *more* rather than fewer professional risks. Consequently, by granting **freedom of professional expression**, today's management must set cost-effective targets for those willing to take on the challenge of manufacturing friendly products. This is a necessity because product designs change rapidly, not yearly, but rather within a period of months.

For example, Acer Electronics of Taiwan has implemented the following ten-month product cycle for their computer technology: three months to design, six months to manufacture, one month to liquidate inventories, and then repeating the cycle. Moreover, Acer and some Korean companies, can accept an American order for computer monitors to be manufactured in Asia and delivered within 60 days. Few American-based companies can duplicate this efficiency.

| *Acer Electronics: Ten-Month Product Cycle* |

Consequently, management must set targets to reduce non-value-added costs by immediately implementing the design of friendly products, friendly to the production arena as well as the service organization. Too many companies must be driven by the demands of the marketplace before they are willing to implement this important change. But if organizations are willing to accept the adage that "necessity is the mother of invention," then many managers will forever be playing catch-up. Everything we do, whether in the arena of business, education, or government, must be done under the managerial theme of *value-added analysis*.

VALUE-ADDED ANALYSIS

VALUE-ADDED ANALYSIS is all-inclusive, from the issuance of purchase orders to the shipment of finished goods and services. Many people have expressed concern about my continuing drive to encourage organizational units to focus on value-added activities. The reason I urge management to move in this direction is simply because the global economy will not permit the inefficiencies that exist today. I firmly believe that we can not sit passively by, but must immediately become more competitive throughout the markets we serve.

Any profitable company that is successful due to advanced technology should immediately embark upon a continuous improvement program. This concept of **continuous improvements** remains a never-ending challenge to all organizations. As an example, if a company has high retained earnings, it has little or no problem obtaining financial letters-of-credit. Borrowing money is easy when one is financially sound. Similarly, I would encourage every profitable organization to borrow professional talent (including outside professionals) to assist in profit maintenance while increasing market share and continuous improvement programs.

In essence, when things are good, make them even better by assigning employees the task of continuous improvements.

Remember, if you are doing things today as you did yesterday, watch out for the competition, because change is so essential to success.

To assure success, management must carefully monitor productivity improvements throughout the organization.

PRODUCTIVITY MEASURES

PRODUCTIVITY MEASURES make effective road maps for management. Unfortunately, many management personnel throughout business, education and government fail to monitor and maintain productivity improvements they have achieved. They neglect implementing continuous improvement programs *throughout* the organization. For instance, manufacturing organizations are continuously challenged to improve, while support groups often linger at the doorstep of ineffectiveness, adding financial burdens to the operating units.

Productivity measures pertain to all functional units within an organization. For example, purchase orders should be monitored quarterly to ascertain reductions of this non-value-added cost. One should ask pertinent questions: What is the cost to issue a purchase order? How many are issued each month? How can this number be reduced? What is management's ultimate target? Are there too many suppliers? What contributions are the suppliers making to reduce this expense? Suppliers will comply if management requests their assistance as strategic partners in driving down non-value-added costs. The accounting department can also be of great assistance. Is there a redundancy in purchasing activity? How about the cost and number of payment checks for goods and services—is there a better way? And what about measuring the logistics and warehousing costs of producing more products than the market can immediately bear? Again, the competitiveness of the new millennium will not permit increasing warehousing costs.

Perhaps management can embark upon a program called *build-to-order*, thereby reducing inventory expenses. And what about the measure of the Management Information System (MIS) group? Chances are they are spending 80 percent of their time maintaining present systems, leaving little time for implementing advancing technologies. Here I firmly believe organizations cannot upgrade MIS systems from within. To remain competitive, they simply must OUTSOURCE (Efficiency Factor #5) this service to a third party. Otherwise they will not maintain a dynamic MIS leadership position and will find themselves with antiquated systems and negative continuous improvements.

Additional productivity measures focus on the output of personnel and equipment. These can be gauged by one of many methods. I prefer units-of-output per employee or revenue per employee per year. The measure of capital investments can be gauged by implementing Total Equipment Productivity. This measures equipment uptime and the implementation of methods to further improve running time with an increase of output. Management should consider these measures in line with directing employees to be more productive under what I call *High-Level Activities.*

HIGH-LEVEL ACTIVITIES

HIGH-LEVEL ACTIVITIES (HLA) are those that result in the highest return to an organization. For example, a top manager should be spending time conceptualizing improvements within the organization rather than wasting valuable hours on plans that should be HLAs for subordinates.

Another way of looking at HLAs is to first focus on the most costly operating procedures. An example here would be the head of accounting asking pertinent questions: Does this department continue to request additional personnel as the organization grows, or should more efficient electronic programs be implemented? The latter is a major HLA for the comptrolling officer. I offer the following HLAs for department heads of respective operating units:
- Purchasing: Reduce the number of purchase orders.
- Materials: Reduce the number of suppliers, inventory levels, and transportation.
- Quality: Eliminate incoming or source inspection.
- Human Resources: Maintain an annual employment matrix, with a window of at least three months lead time prior to hiring a new employee.
- Engineering: Reduce model changeover time.
- Design: Commit to manufacturing friendly products.
- Production: Implement integrated manufacturing because it provides for direct shipments, and focus on built-to-order products.

HLAs define the order of commitment in an organization's efforts to maintain continuous improvements.

X-MATRIX

X-MATRIX provides one final, comprehensive tool for gaining *The Competitive Edge.* A scientific method, X-MATRIX provides means for planning, implementing, and monitoring the effectiveness of HLAs as well as other ways of improving profitability.

X-MATRIX incorporates a four-part plan to define objectives, items, targets, and the realized gain from each group's commitment. It further determines the responsible department, schedules implementation, and monitors progress. The X-MATRIX chart (Appendix A) is prepared simultaneously with a new business plan. It is most successful when the highest ranking officer sets the general targeted goals, say a 35 percent improvement across the board, by spelling out the needs of each of the functional departments.

Next, the second level of command can more precisely define the objectives and items of their respective units; e.g., to achieve a 35 percent reduction in non-value-added costs associated with the issuance of purchase orders. In the same manner, managers, supervisors, and clerical staff can continue to be more definitive because of their hands-on-involvement with the details required to reach the reduction goal.

Once a month, perhaps during monthly financial meetings, respective department heads report on the success or failure of their implemented actions. It is important to have each functional department make a presentation so as not to discourage the doers from thinking others are not as committed.

There is one significant challenge with this method of measurement. X-MATRIX is as close to a scientific, business-planning tool as one will find. Consequently, the discipline of all involved parties can either make or break the program's success. The only way to prevent failure is for top management to continue to demonstrate a strong interest.

As we continue with *The Competitive Edge,* I will introduce additional monitoring programs to assist managers like you in your drive for continuous improvements. One such program, which will be further defined, is the Efficiency Factors Organizational Plan (Appendix C). This chart is a controlling plan, similar to an organization chart, for implementing and monitoring the Eight Efficiency Factors by naming a chairperson, (usually from top management), to head the organization, and chairpersons to direct each of the eight factors. It is the task of each of the nine members to encourage everyone to move forward, secure in the knowledge that they have the **freedom to innovate without fear of failure.**

This program is designed to assist management in selecting and empowering key personnel to be responsible for guiding various teams in their constant drive for **continuous improvements.**

Now that we have laid the management groundwork, we can continue our exciting journey of implementing the Eight Efficiency Factors for *The Competitive Edge.*

HUMAN RESOURCES
"THE GUIDING PRINCIPLE"

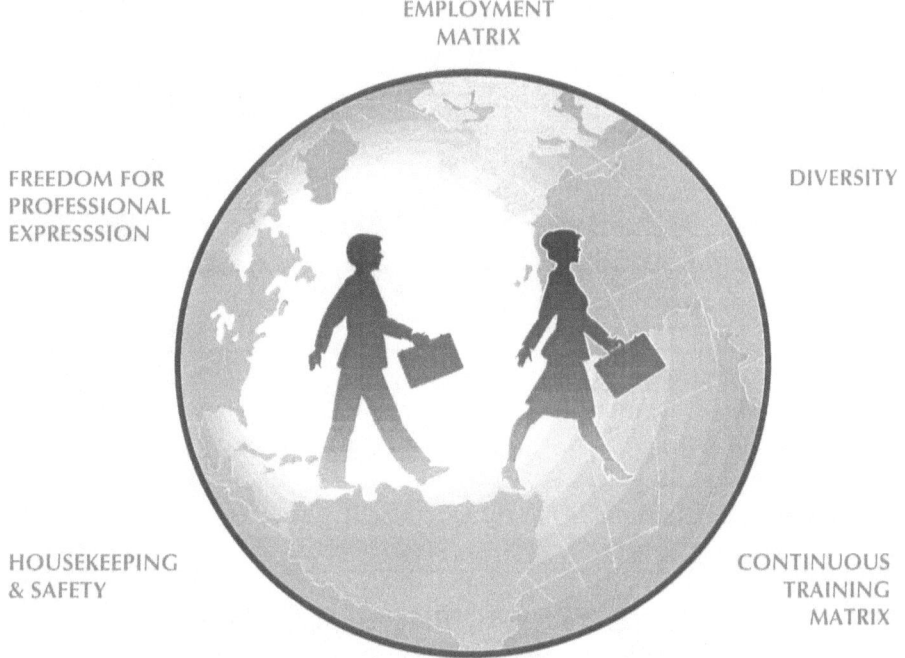

EMPLOYMENT
MATRIX

FREEDOM FOR
PROFESSIONAL
EXPRESSSION

DIVERSITY

HOUSEKEEPING
& SAFETY

CONTINUOUS
TRAINING
MATRIX

CHANGE... SO ESSENTIAL TO SUCCESS

LOOK BEYOND THE COMPLEXION
OF THE INDIVIDUAL TO FIND THE
TRUE WORTH.

FREEDOM TO INNOVATE
WITHOUT FEAR OF FAILURE

THE COMPETITIVE EDGE

Joseph J. McHugh

Efficiency Factor #1
HUMAN RESOURCES

In this chapter:
√ **Employee Empowerment**
√ **Job Consolidation**
√ **Interpersonal Skills**
√ **Challenging Individual Capabilities**
√ **Employment of "Temps"**

Exploring HUMAN RESOURCES as Efficiency Factor #1 provides the first leg of our voyage towards competitiveness in the new millennium. *People* form the foundation for any successful business, education, or government organization. *People* select and process materials, operate machinery, discharge waste into the environment, and educate and govern other employees. Consequently, management teams must increase their commitment to the selection, training, and retention of this most important resource.

Within any organization, a clear mission statement sets efficient and positive standards for HUMAN RESOURCES:

We will use professional and ethical practices in the hiring and orientation of our employees. All workers must possess the skills and work ethic necessary for the company to be a good community citizen, recognized by other organizations as a worthy competitor. Employees will be provided with continuous training to improve skills which support advancing technologies.

When I refer to *employees or workers* I am talking in heterogeneous terms, because people from all cultures are crossing borders and entering into world-wide business, education, and government organizations at an escalating rate. Multinational companies are also expanding their frontiers at a similar pace. Because of the vast market for their products, emerging nations, though homogeneous today, will soon match other countries in cultural complexity, and this escalating diversity will create increasing challenges for management. There is, however, a plus side: diversity within the work force offers personnel an opportunity to learn from one another by gaining a better understanding of various cultures. The commingling of nationalities within the work force provides a continuing awareness of others, thereby reducing internal tensions and conflicts.

Today, managers and workers alike must **look beyond the complexion of the individual and assess his or her true capabilities.** Most organizations already have a diverse population striving toward common goals. Consequently, managers are challenged to direct and motivate diverse employees effectively at all levels. Perhaps the surest avenue of opportunity comes through *employee empowerment,* which unleashes the talents and creative input of many people.

EMPLOYEE EMPOWERMENT

Employee empowerment opens possibilities for both workers and management. Management sets the boundaries and targets, encouraging various teams to extend their talents in the quest for continuous improvements. It is important to note that managers do not give up their right to manage. As organizational conditions change, management simply sets new boundaries and targets.

When introducing *employee empowerment,* you must realize that not everyone will embrace it, for some will always resist any kind of change. The majority of employees, however, will welcome new opportunities and take ownership of their jobs and organization if they are professionally guided by management. This guidance, of course, stands as the cornerstone for the program's success.

Employee empowerment also offers tremendous opportunities for **freedom of professional expression.** I have found that for the program to be effective, managers must provide visible and continuing encouragement. To the vast number of employees, empowerment provides a chance to become more involved in decision-making. Since the days of Maslow, we have recognized that physical needs, once satisfied, are short-lived. But for humans, the freedom of professional expression satisfies powerful psychological needs and the individual drive for self-actualization.

3

During a recent "burger" price war, Southern California's In-N-Out Burgers did not lower their prices, yet maintained a steady flow of satisfied customers. Whether intentional or not, this fast-food chain offers an excellent example of employee empowerment. Since its inception, the company's management has encouraged employees to exercise maximum efficiency as they serve customers with a smile.

> *In-N-Out Burgers:*
> *Employee*
> *Empower-*
> *ment in Action*

When an order is place at an In-N-Out Burgers drive-through microphone, the individual taking the order is the same person who handles its transfer and payment. He or she notes the request and communicates it to cooks who prepare the food from scratch. While the burgers are on the grill, the order-taker fixes the drinks and dispatches the entire meal within minutes.

It's fun to watch employees (with no visible supervision) share a common excitement in filling each new order on time. In-N-Out Burgers has no food freezers on the premises, which means that meat and vegetables are brought in fresh each day. This fresh-food situation demands close cooperation between employees and embodies the *build-to-order* concept that I will mention later. If a fast-food chain can motivate low-wage employees to higher levels of performance, why then should it be so difficult for management in other industries to meet the challenge?

The implementation of an *employee empowerment* program must be designed with supportive targets, time-lines, measures, and adequate financial investment. As redesign teams smooth out the resistance-to-change mentality, cells or silos will start to tumble, and levels of management will, over time, begin to shrink. If properly encouraged by management, *employee empowerment* offers a way to correct managerial sins of the past, while offering exciting prospects for future gains.

Because management is an art, historically some managers have implemented certain HUMAN RESOURCES policies and procedures that were not always in the best interest of the organization. For example, even today, organizational structures invite far too many titles and job classifications. The dynamic global economy of the future will dictate a reduction of the hierarchy.

GLOBAL ECONOMY

Many organizations are downsizing, restructuring, and offering early-out programs. These reductions present a serious challenge because in some cases the loss of valuable personnel drains the organization of talent necessary to meet the challenges of the new millennium. In the future, society will shoulder the burden of fewer jobs coupled with lesser-paying positions. At present, solutions are elusive and therefore challenge the economy's continuing growth. Sadly, we can no longer afford our present level of affluence.

> Talent Drain

Job elimination causes both corporate and personal hardships as employees cope with title changes and transfers to new positions. Unfortunately, with the challenges of a global economy, management personnel have no alternative but to correct their predecessors' mistakes. To be globally competitive, we can no longer accept the inertia of the past or the inefficiencies of the present. Unfortunately, this necessary management shift will result in employee casualties, the ultimate price of past management's lack of business foresight. Today's top management must recognize the need to constantly improve their business practices and not allow poor adaptation to cause consolidations or shutdowns at the local level. Any company remaining static will lose its competitive edge, causing management to take note of diminishing returns. Let's explore several efficiency proposals involving HUMAN RESOURCES.

> Continuous
> Improvements

JOB CONSOLIDATION

First, given the present employment level, managers should freeze employment and consolidate jobs, especially in the non-value-added functions. Managers frequently believe that they need additional personnel to deal with expanding responsibilities, but this is simply not true. Far too often employees get in each other's way because they have too much idle time. When employees are not utilizing their true capabilities, the result is **under**-employment.

In the initial phase, *job consolidation* may cause unrest, but in the long run both management and employees will enjoy more personal fulfillment recognition. Too often people wait to be given additional responsibility. I encourage employees everywhere to stretch the boundaries of their job definition and become more productive. In other words, individuals should be encouraged to assess their personal skills and take initiative, rather than waiting for specific direction.

INTERPERSONAL SKILLS

Interpersonal skills remain the driving force behind success. Those who exercise initiative without such skills will quickly be diminished in the eyes of their colleagues, becoming the proverbial bull-in-the-china-shop. An employee's image, formed through his or her *interpersonal skills*, can be a tremendous asset in future career moves, or it can become a lasting negative, unless new employment offers a second chance. Managers have the responsibility to inspire their employees' direction and drive by guiding their behavior. In this area many supervisors simply fail to discuss what they perceive as an individual's shortcomings. Consequently, the employee continues to perform to everyone's displeasure.

CHALLENGING INDIVIDUAL CAPABILITIES

To *challenge individual capabilities,* managers must help employees to grow within the organization, rather than limiting them. Too often, managers focus on an individual's weaknesses, when in reality, he or she could contribute far more if not hindered by such short-sighted views. As managers we must test employees' true potential by extending challenges and performance levels beyond our preconceptions. Time and again I've observed managers recruit too many people to perform a given task, when they should be starting with the minimum number. **It's easy to hire, but difficult to fire!**

For example, when a special task surfaces to deal with a problem such as incorrect packaging, the tendency is to call in temporary help. But why not go to the administrative staff and request their assistance? I call this the *tiger team*: employees willing to go that extra mile to help the company maintain profitability.

EMPLOYMENT OF "TEMPS"

Employment of temporary help is something more and more companies are now doing in an effort to reduce overhead. I support this practice when production needs are limited, or when manual tasks are so redundant as to create avoidance. However, in many cases, the hiring of temporary help is what I call a "license to steal." Once a manager agrees to open the floodgates to temporary hiring, the conceptual skills of those in charge are soon lost. It becomes too easy to say, "Hey, Charlie's out today. Get somebody in here!" When employees are absent, especially non-value-added personnel, we're frequently better off depending on our in-house staff to fill the void.

Given expanding market demand, however, management will usually approve the hiring of additional personnel. The orientation, training, and retention of new employees must be planned carefully, because HUMAN RESOURCES is truly the most important Efficiency Factor. Those chartered with the task of screening new hires must assure management of each individual's capabilities, **before** they are interviewed within the targeted department or division. Many times resumés are passed on without proper screening. In anticipation of employment needs, each functional department should prepare an annual *employment matrix*, forecasting, as accurately as possible, the number of employees to be hired, coupled with the respective discipline.

EMPLOYMENT MATRIX

The annual *employment matrix* needs to be updated monthly and then implemented by the Human Resources department. When compiling these data, managers should base potential employment needs on attrition and demand forecast following a job-consolidation program. The *employment matrix* can be further enhanced, especially for non-technical positions, by providing a *rolling employment* schedule. Rolling employment is a concept of screening potential employees without the immediate intention of hiring. This practice provides an inventory of potential employees ready to meet the organization's future needs. Following the screening, management should approve the employment of a small team of non-technical personnel | *Rolling Employment* | who would be committed to advanced training according to the organization's needs. When a position becomes available, the respective employees will at least have completed basic training and can then, on a moment's notice, transfer to their respective department. Too often we wait for terminations before we hire, and then panic at the cry, "We need someone NOW!" Hiring under duress often results in a mismatch of employee needs to the position's requirements.

Here again, job consolidation must be completed first in order to ascertain true employment needs. Hiring is a weighty decision, and employee retention should be foremost in your mind, coupled with a long-range forecast supporting all additional personnel. If we were to hire on a "cradle-to-grave" basis, we would be far more careful about which and how many employees we hired. One final point: the hiring of technical personnel takes at least three months from the time the need arises; therefore, the *employment matrix* can add efficiency to this important factor of productivity.

CONCLUSION

Personnel, I'd wager, is the highest cost to most if not all organizations. Consequently, HUMAN RESOURCES is the key to continuing business success. Efficient HUMAN RESOURCES practices assist in maintaining good housekeeping and safety; they provide training and motivational programs because employees need to feel good about themselves to be productive. Continuing education and training becomes more and more essential for employees to work with ADVANCING TECHNOLOGIES (Efficiency Factor # 6). And above all, efficient personnel practices must guard against too many titles and positions.

Today, management comprises three tiers of experience. First we have the pre-baby boomer generation, composed for the most part of today's decision makers because they have reached the top positions. The infamous baby

| *Three Tiers of Experience* |

boomers are what I call the cross-over business generation. They grew up in affluence, and fortunately or unfortunately, have had to learn later in life how to work harder to retain that prosperity. The last tier is what I perceive to be the most important; they are the post-baby boomers, the computer generation. These young people possess the knowledge we desperately need to navigate the information highway and propel us into the new millennium. This generation must be given the freedom of professional expression to extend their knowledge across all business functions, for they are the ones who best understand the need for continuous improvements, the need to excel, and the need to compete in the global economy.

MATERIALS
EFFICIENCY FACTOR #2

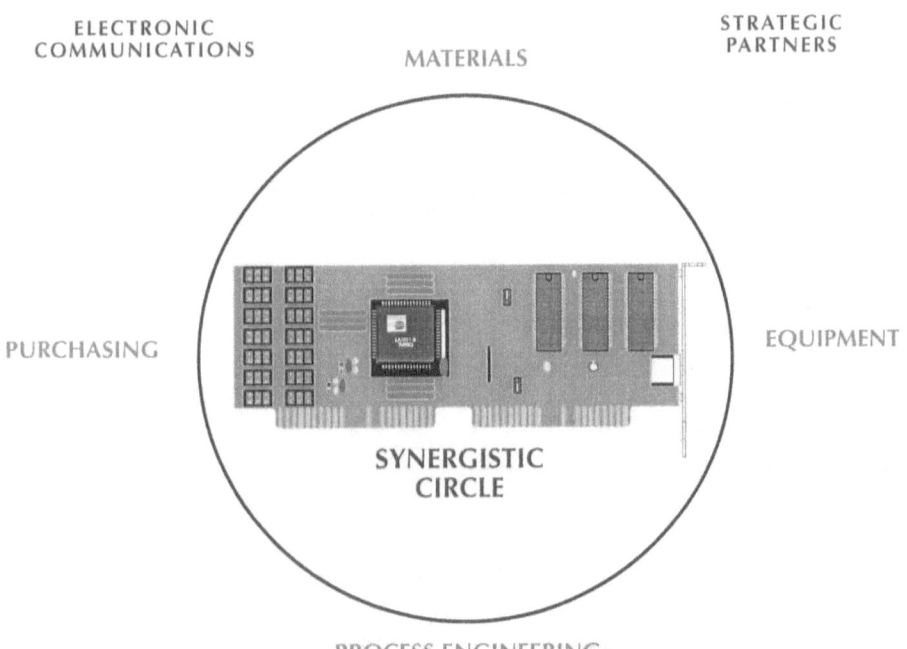

SUPPLIER
SELECTION

ELECTRONIC
COMMUNICATIONS

MATERIALS

STRATEGIC
PARTNERS

PURCHASING

EQUIPMENT

SYNERGISTIC
CIRCLE

PROCESS ENGINEERING

NON - VALUE - ADDED COSTS
(SELF INVOICING)

WASTE MINIMIZATION

THE COMPETITIVE EDGE

Joseph J. McHugh

Efficiency Factor #2
MATERIALS

In this chapter:
√ **Supplier Selection**
√ **Synergy of Supplier and User**
√ **Direct Materials**
√ **Indirect Materials**
√ **MRO Materials**
√ **Eliminating Purchase Orders**

Traveling toward our goal of *The Competitive Edge* requires careful navigation through deep and costly waters of operating expenses. Next to employee expense, MATERIALS loom as the second highest operating expense on our journey to profitability. Consequently, we must pay significant attention to the efficiency of this expensive resource, from issuance of purchase orders to final shipments of finished goods or services.

Within education and government organizations, MATERIALS consist primarily of administrative supplies, employee needs, leasehold improvements, and maintenance. MATERIALS used in business, however, include direct and indirect materials, maintenance, repair, and operating supplies. As a consequence, I will, for the most part, focus on production functions as I outline changes necessary to reduce this costly Efficiency Factor.

SUPPLIER SELECTION

Supplier selection is essential to improving MATERIALS efficiencies. A supplier committed to "strategic partnering," working collectively with the equipment manufacturer and the processing engineer, can effectively increase material yields, reduce negative discharges to the environment, and subsequently improve the overall profitability of the organization. Simultaneously, supplier-user synergy can significantly reduce non-value-added costs associated with all phases of administration and logistics support. Purchase orders must eventually be replaced by using a production schedule and electronic data interchange. The service industry has far surpassed other industries in implementing the electronic transfer of information. *Speed* will be the buzz word of the future. Consequently, anything not adding value to the flow of materials, from purchase order, to receipt of goods, to final shipment of finished goods and services will continue to challenge productivity improvements. Eliminating these invisible cost drains is **the** greatest opportunity for continuous improvements, offering increased profitability. *Do it Now!*

Prior to selecting a supplier, you should visit their operations to determine their commitment to be the highest quality supplier with limited overhead, inventories, and personnel but excellent quality control. Just touring suppliers' facilities will give you a feel for the effectiveness of their management. Is

> *Strategic Partnering*

housekeeping in order? (Poor housekeeping generates handling defects.) Are employees focused on their respective tasks? Is the building design and construction far beyond the needs of present operations? Is there un-utilized space? Is the management staff too large? A "yes" answer to many of these simple questions indicates that the cost of their products or service is noncompetitive or very shortly will be. Later I will comment on the value of strategic partnering between supplier and user. For now, let it suffice to say that the elements, constituents, and substances of materials are obviously significant when worked into a more finished form. Limited interchange between supplier and user must improve because the future, if not today, will demand supplier-user synergy to boost productivity, including both environmental and cost improvements.

DIRECT MATERIALS

Today numerous laboratories focus on MATERIALS research. But this focus cannot remain parochial; research must be shared with the users, either the manufacturer or the end user. Perhaps the greatest return to all parties is in the *direct materials* category. As the term implies, direct materials, after processing, become part of the finished goods. To be efficient and cost effective with direct materials, we need the collective synergy of the material and equipment suppliers and the respective processing engineer. But most companies fail in reaping the benefits of this dynamic opportunity for continuous improvements.

In this regard, material suppliers must assist users in achieving higher materials efficiencies at the point of use. No longer will the competitive global economy permit inefficiency of materials and the subsequent loss of sales and profitability. Suppliers cannot hope to sit back selling more and more materials to inefficient users. They must become proactive by monitoring the efficiency levels of their own materials. I fail to understand why material suppliers do not become more involved with the equipment supplier and the processing engineer to increase the efficiency of their own materials. By so doing, everyone gains; limited materials resources are protected, the waste discharge to the environment is reduced, and the quality of the finished product is enhanced. All of these benefits lead to greater customer satisfaction.

Regarding the issue of environmental regulations, the material supplier has the responsibility to assure all parties of proper governmental compliance, especially such requirements as those of the Toxic Substance Control Act (TSCA), ie., the composition of the material must be registered prior to distribution. On the other hand, the purchasing department of the user must challenge the supplier about their compliance because the end result rests with the user. Consequently, supplier and purchasing departments have a dual responsibility with regard to governmental compliance. Regulations pertain not only to domestic materials, but foreign material suppliers as well. Many times we take for granted the compliance level of foreign suppliers and by so doing forget that the burden of proof rests with the user.

> *Environmental Regulations*

The increasing environmental awareness of many governments will continue to place the burden of responsibility directly on the user, followed reluctantly by the material supplier. Today, for the most part, material suppliers cannot provide the environmental consequences of using their materials. Their reasoning is "we don't know the manufacturing process." This narrow view must change, and the only one who can encourage positive change is the management of the user. Collectively, the supplier and user must identify any atmospheric Volatile Organic Compound (VOC) discharges to determine whether or not current levels are in compliance or if any subsequent increase of VOCs will exceed permitted levels. Of equal importance are the Threshold Limit Values (employee inhalation safety levels). Will a change in material composition exceed the employee safety level or for that matter, reduce it? The buzz phase here is *waste minimization*. The efficiencies and subsequent discharges of various materials will continue to place added responsibilities on the supplier-user relationship. It would, therefore, be in the best interest of both parties to combine synergistic forces to set targets and timetables for waste minimization.

INDIRECT MATERIALS

Another element in this drive for MATERIALS efficiencies is limiting indirect material usage. Indirect materials are necessary to support the processing of direct materials but are not part of the finished product. These materials are non-value-added because they add nothing to the finished product. As non-value-added materials, management has the sole responsibility of monitoring the costs associated with indirect materials. An example of indirect materials would be oils and cleaning supplies. As with direct materials, efficiency and environmental responsibilities rest with both the supplier and the user. Too many times indirect materials are not given the same management control as direct materials. Here, again stands an opportunity for you to set targets and timetables for reduction of these non-value-added costs.

I believe many hidden costs are associated with indirect materials. Each production unit should conduct a self-examination of the uses of those almost-invisible indirect materials. For example, are we using the right oil weight? Is the cleaning solution right for the job, given the fair market price? In fact, the costs are so well hidden that outsourcing might be in a manufacturer's best interests. Most operating units are committed to *direct* material and productivity efficiencies. By outsourcing the efficiency of *indirect* materials, you would select a "general" supplier to study the numerous indirect material functions and, for a fee, implement programs for the reduction of these non-value-added costs. Finally, you might question if the material suppliers are aware of the utilization of indirect materials. My belief is that operating units unilaterally select the indirect material supplier without proper assistance from the purchasing department.

As is true for direct materials, Material Safety Data Sheets (MSDS) are required for indirect materials. Purchasing personnel stand as the first line of defense in protecting the organization from violations of this OSHA mandate. Unfortunately, many times operating units solicit materials samples from suppliers without regard for the responsibility of purchasing. The supplier, for example, should be held accountable for any and all test materials. Following the testing of materials, the supplier must accept responsibility for the removal of unused materials. Many times the process engineer simply passes the disposal of indirect materials onto the maintenance or waste treatment activities. By doing so, non-value-added costs increase without the knowledge of management. This becomes another hidden cost that diminishes profits. The fine line between indirect supplies and maintenance, repair, and operation supplies continues to confuse many people, especially in the case of oils, grease and so on, the subject of my last category of materials.

MRO SUPPLIES

Maintenance, Repair, and Operating (MRO) supplies are the backbone of operating units because, without maintenance, especially preventative maintenance, productivity will suffer. This is also true of repair and operating supplies. The latter includes the materials necessary for employees to complete their assigned tasks. This grouping of materials can run into millions of dollars of non-value-added costs. Here again, unless managers like you indicate an interest, this cost will increase at an alarming rate each year. Many times managers turn blind eyes to this ever-increasing cost because keeping the equipment running is of paramount concern. I agree; however, I fear that these non-value-added costs are increasing year after year without proper control. I believe MRO supplies should be attacked from zero-base budgeting. Forget what it was last year; rather consider what the competitive edge will permit today and tomorrow in a global economy. This is why I feel so strongly about the synergy required between the material provider, equipment supplier, and the processing engineer.

Later we will offer guide lines pertaining to EQUIPMENT, ENVIRONMENT and NON-VALUE-ADDED COST reductions (Efficiency Factors 3, 4, and 7). However, at the risk of being redundant later, some thoughts on this subject are in order. Materials suppliers play an even greater role when it comes to the non-value-added costs associated with the transfer and inventory of materials. Today, the global economy simply will not permit the level of non-value-added costs associated with material purchases, freight forwarding, and inventories. More and more we need strategic partnering to collectively seek continuous improvements in reducing all costs associated with materials. In the immediate future, production facilities will only be competitive if they *build to order*. What this very simply means is that mass production, inventory, and shipping are too much of a financial burden because all these costs are, you guessed it, non-value-added.

The issuance of purchase orders, revisions, and so on has become simply an administrative, antiquated jumble of paper work. In the case of line production, the production schedule can very simply serve as the purchase order, except the accounting department may object. But, hey, we are talking competitiveness within a global economy. **You may remember that if you are doing things today, as you did yesterday, your competition is sailing right by you.** Looking at this guideline very simplistically, the production schedule tells the supplier the user's plan. It then becomes the supplier's responsibility to send the respective materials to the off-loading dock when needed. FOB purchases suggest a weakness in this guideline because the user pays for materials at the supplier's dock. What a sin! What incentive does the material supplier have in helping the user reduce freight and warehousing costs when payment is made prior to shipment, and as a consequence the user pays for freight and warehousing? I will offer more on this subject later.

CONCLUSION

In tackling this important MATERIALS Efficiency Factor, you as managers must challenge *all* costs associated with the purchase of *all* materials. Review your supplier base and question the number of suppliers because the more suppliers the more non-value-added costs. Refuse any costs associated with incoming material inspection or source inspections because these costs are truly the responsibility of the supplier. Pull the supplier into your synergistic circle to help you be more competitive. Challenge the financial waste associated with purchasing, freight, warehousing, as well as environmental non-value-added costs. With MATERIALS as the second most expensive part of the operational budget, the supplier can, if requested, help in *The Competitive Edge* in this challenging global economy.

EQUIPMENT EFFICIENCY FACTOR #3

ENVIRONMENTAL
RELEASES

ADVANCING
TECHNOLOGY

EQUIPMENT

MANUFACTURE
FRIENDLY PRODUCTS

PURCHASING

MATERIALS

PROCESS ENGINEER

PUSH-BUTTON
TECHNOLOGY

INTEGRATED
MANUFACTURING

THE COMPETITIVE EDGE

Joseph J. McHugh

Efficiency Factor #3
EQUIPMENT

In this chapter:
√ **Total Equipment Productivity**
√ **Green-Light Analysis**
√ **Turnkey Systems**
√ **Push-Button Technology**
√ **Manufacturing Friendly Products**
√ **Cell Assembly**

After HUMAN RESOURCES and MATERIALS, the third leg of our journey toward competitive production involves making sound decisions about EQUIPMENT. Equipment purchases to support advancing technology require major capital outlay. Equipment investments, therefore, entail significant risks because of the uncertainty of the expanding market place. Consequently, supportive engineering studies and financial documentation must be thorough and convincing so that you can reasonably assess the potential profit return of new equipment purchases.

In this section of our journey of discovery, we will explore guidelines for evaluating present equipment capabilities, purchasing turnkey systems and push-button technology, and manufacturing friendly products. I will also discuss how to reduce equipment investments by implementing cell assembly versus conveyorized production.

Prior to committing to additional equipment investment dollars, you must first and foremost determine the true capabilities of your present equipment. For example, analyze the effects of increasing the speeds of the present equipment or reducing the space between work stations. This analysis can best be done by using the measure of *total equipment productivity* or TEP.

TOTAL EQUIPMENT PRODUCTIVITY

The TEP associated with today's level of technology must be maximized by using the synergy of equipment manufacturers, material suppliers, and process engineers. Too often engineering and management teams believe they can justify equipment investments based solely on their expertise, without input from materials and equipment specialists. I propose we change our thinking on this subject by committing to an open discussion with all involved parties. When demand is nearing production limitations, line personnel usually request equipment modifications based on their own experience after perhaps only limited discussions with equipment suppliers. This request for costly modifications or additions is based on present material yields and parameter settings by the processing engineer. I propose that all future equipment studies be collectively supported by all three parties: representatives, materials suppliers, and process engineers.

The process engineer must first assure management of the maximum yield and output of the present equipment settings given the current level of technology. To achieve maximum material yields, materials suppliers should be involved because they have the best knowledge of the composition of the materials and any factors that might limit or expand the efficiency of the materials. Certainly this need suggests that the user must request technical support from the material supplier beyond the level of sales representatives. Moreover, | *Synergy* | what about the support of the equipment manufacturer? Shouldn't the engineering staff request information from this untapped resource? Equipment manufacturers should know how to increase speeds, how to adjust the equipment for maximum output, and so on. Without belaboring the point, my guideline would be for a closer unity between the equipment and materials suppliers and the process engineer before committing to new equipment investments. As an experienced operational manager, I challenge you to test this synergistic concept. You will immediately observe productivity improvements that will encourage across-the-board implementation of this dynamic program. Following this comprehensive study, request a complete analysis of the true capabilities of the present equipment prior to the expenditure of additional financing. This additional analysis can best be achieved by what I label the *green-light method of analysis.*

The *green-light method of analysis* is a stop-and-go review of the requirements leading to the final investment commitment for new equipment. The first green light or go signal is a complete review of the full capabilities of the present equipment complement. Here you must ask yourself the TEP (Total Equipment Productivity) measure: Is it 60, 70, or 90 percent? If the answer is not in line with your acceptable standards, what can be done to further increase up time? Many questions should be asked at this junction: Can the speeds of the present equipment be increased? Can stations be moved closer together? Is material shrinkage too high? Are model changeovers too frequent or too lengthy? Are we producing in volume, hoping for continued customer support, or is the equipment capable of *integrated manufacturing* i.e., the processing capability to produce different models in tandem to support day-to-day market demand? Can the work week be extended? This latter question is extremely important because of the expenses of advancing technologies. Since technology changes so fast, new equipment may be antiquated before its time. If the lifetime of your present equipment can be extended by simply lengthening the work week, then the company can delay costly new equipment purchases. If you are content with the analysis thus far, then the light is green permitting you to move to the next junction.

The next step in the *green light analysis* is your study of return on investment or ROI. Here you must define your time period and level of ROI. Under this step of the financial analysis, the equipment cost must include transportation, installation, space, and taxation. Should you be satisfied with this study, then you have a *green light* and move on to the next junction.

The next *green light* review requires assessing the true technical capabilities of your in-house technical staff. With today's complex technology, how does your

Technical Competence

company maintain the level of technical competence necessary to effectively utilize the modernization of present equipment as well as the installation of advancing technologies? This I perceive to be one of your greatest challenges. You may recall, earlier I offered the idea that **if you are doing things today as you did yesterday, your competition is passing you right by.** Any management that is not providing continual technical training cannot expect to maintain the level of technical competence necessary to cope with the rapid changes taking place in the global economy. Many companies in Asia are going so far as providing technical schools at their various plant sites. Continual training of a technical staff will truly challenge the competitive level of American companies. If, however, you are content with the expertise of your current technical staff, then the light is green, and you may move to the next junction.

Next, environmental considerations must be addressed both by local line management and technical staff to protect your business from serious liabilities associated with non-compliances. Here again, you as managers must request the support of the equipment manufacturer, material supplier, and the processing engineer.

Let's review, what I believe to be, the responsibility of each of these representatives.

| *Environmental* |
| *Considerations* |

The equipment supplier has the collective responsibility to ascertain environmental discharges into the atmosphere, ground, or water. Far too many times the equipment manufacturer fails to offer assistance in designing environmental discharge devices to help reduce pollution. Their reasoning is their lack of knowledge about the composition of the materials or the process setting of the equipment. This position can be altered if local management has the commitment to employ the knowledge of this vast resource-the equipment specialists-before committing to major equipment investments.

Next the materials suppliers must be called upon to offer the engineers knowledge about potential environmental discharges associated with their materials. Suppliers know the compositions of their materials and are better prepared to offer advice once they have an understanding of the processing parameters. I have experience working with materials suppliers who helped reduce atmospheric discharges simply by changing the chemical composition of their materials. The local processing engineer must be encouraged to call upon this untapped source of knowledge—the materials supplier—rather than going it alone.

Yet the processing engineer is, quite frankly, the key to the success of environmental waste reduction. The setting of the equipment parameters to maintain material efficiencies is the primary charter of this position. But the synergy of both the materials and equipment suppliers provides the engineering department with the knowledge to increase material and equipment efficiencies, as well as

| *Process Engineer:* |
| *The Key* |

providing safeguards to protect the environment. Remember that environmental discharges are costly and non-value-added. Following the collective input of these three disciplines, then you can give the *green light* for the purchase of equipment. But the final commitment to invest in new equipment requires further *green light analysis* about the most cost-effective type of installation.

When purchasing equipment, you as managers must weigh the value of *turnkey* versus self installation. Often managers believe that in-house technicians and maintenance can complete the installation. I disagree with this position, especially with regard to high-tech equipment. Once your company elects to install new equipment, the equipment manufacturers' level of risk is dramatically reduced. The warranty is negated because, "we did not install the equipment" or "you changed the design." My reason for advising *turnkey systems* is that the method of payments can be controlled and dependent on proof-of-performance. I suggest implementing a five-step method of payment, with each step based on proof-of-performance:

• Step 1: 20% payment with purchase order.
• Step 2: 20% payment after electrical/mechanical check out.
• Step 3: 20% payment after equipment optimization or ascertaining all the parameter settings as defined in the purchase order.
• Step 4: 20% payment after the processing of prove-in materials.
• Step 5: 20% payment after a defined proof-of-performance such as five days of successful processing to the specifications and design of the equipment. An example of this would be achieving specified speeds and yields.

Once the proof-of-performance is successful, the light is green again and you move to the final junction: determining the necessary information to maintain the equipment in the future.

These ancillary items should be part of every contract for new equipment:
• 1. Proper safety interlocks, especially for foreign-made equipment (e.g., lock-out-tag-out features)
• 2. Three equipment manuals to be provided upon receipt of the equipment
• 3. A list of spare parts and the purchase of same
• 4. Technical support and training by the equipment supplier during and after installation
• 5. Annual preventive maintenance contracts, if desirable.
• 6. Maximum warranty period
• 7. Equipment drawings on computer disks

I believe the *green-light* guide leading to the purchase of new equipment will become an excellent tool because the check points along the way provide a clear vision of EQUIPMENT, an important and costly factor of production.

PUSH-BUTTON TECHNOLOGY

Another avenue for maximizing equipment efficiency is what I call *push-button technology*. This concept provides the technical capability for line employees to adjust the parameter setting at their respective stations when model changes are introduced. In the past management was content to fund the employment of a technical staff to provide assistance for what was believed to be too technical in nature for the line operators. Today, with the competitive demands of a global economy, you cannot continue to support this non-value added cost. The parameter setting of the equipment must be designed to permit line employees to "push a button" to make the adjustment, especially for electronic settings. Here again, this concept must be built into the construction of the equipment, rather than a costly modification to the equipment at a later date.

MANUFACTURING FRIENDLY PRODUCTS

To further enhance this capability, I offer the guideline of what I call *manufacturing friendly products*. What this entails is the engineering staff considering, more than ever before, designing products for efficient methods of assembly. The number of assembly parts must be reduced with each new design. One illustrative example would be plastic parts. Plastic has memory. Consequently, metal screws should be eliminated as much as possible. The fewer the number of parts, the fewer hand tools, the less energy, fewer people, and so on. Today, companies search the world over for cheap labor. If the product were *manufacturing friendly*, perhaps the finished product could be assembled within the markets served. Often the hidden logistics, warehousing, and administration costs can be far more expensive than the actual assembly costs. And with the rapid design changes taking place, it would seem to me that a first priority of product design would be *manufacturing friendly*. Designing products for ease of assembly can reduce capital equipment investments in the future.

Similarly, in the production and assembly of finished goods, you as managers must look into a continuing reduction of floor space and conveyors because of the allocation costs associated with some of these non-value-added costs. Given a program of *Do-It-Now*, management can entice all employees to assist in the reduction of this cost. Process and industrial engineers should depend more on the capability of line workers to do more, rather than providing table levelers, small space-consuming conveyors, and so on. Indexing conveyors can be replaced by simply asking line employees to manually move products. This seems like an insignificant cost, but when you add the cost of utilities and maintenance, you could readily seek better avenues of improvement. Conveyors, especially lengthy conveyors, can sometimes be more costly than manual performance because with a lengthy conveyor the cost increases dramatically if one station breaks down and 50 other employees are waiting. This subject of conveyors takes us to the last idea pertaining to the EQUIPMENT Efficiency Factor. Today, driven by Asia, many are questioning the value of conveyor-type assembly lines versus what is referred to as *cell assembly*.

CELL ASSEMBLY

Cell assembly is something Maxwell Taylor (the creator of industrial engineering) would disagree with. The cell concept encourages the line operator to do more tasks, even to the extent of totally assembling and testing, rather than continuing to do the same redundant tasks day in and day out. Line employees have the professional talent to do much more than mindless line assembly. And by doing more, they can contribute to the **continuous improvements** so important to management. Quality improves as well as productivity. Moreover, expensive equipment downtime and preventative maintenance expenses drop dramatically because under the cell concept conveyors just might be eliminated. At any rate, given a drive for manufacturing friendly products, the cell method of assembly just might be the order of the day. Certainly, by the elimination of conveyors and associated equipment, the environment both within the work area as well as the community will be improved.

CONCLUSION

Rapidly advancing technologies will continue to diminish returns on investments because product redesigning will occur more frequently. Therefore, the third Efficiency Factor, EQUIPMENT, requires skillful management and new thinking in order to achieve competitive production. The *Green-Light Analysis* of equipment needs encourages you to challenge capital equipment requests. Prior to committing to the purchase of new equipment, consider increasing speeds or extending the work week in order to maximize present equipment capabilities. Employ the synergy of the materials suppler, equipment manufacturer, and the process engineer both to improve *Total Equipment Productivity* and limit environmental discharges. Purchase or upgrade equipment with *push-button technology,* allowing line operators to make rapid electronic adjustments during model changes. Order *turnkey systems* and a proof-of-performance payment plan to place more risk on the equipment manufacturer and less on your company. Design and *manufacture friendly products* to decrease assembly costs. Incorporate *integrated manufacturing* in order to produce different model sizes in tandem. And finally demand continual training in advancing technology for the internal technical staff. These are the keys to achieving a competitive edge with the EQUIPMENT Efficiency Factor.

ENVIRONMENT
EFFICIENCY FACTOR #4

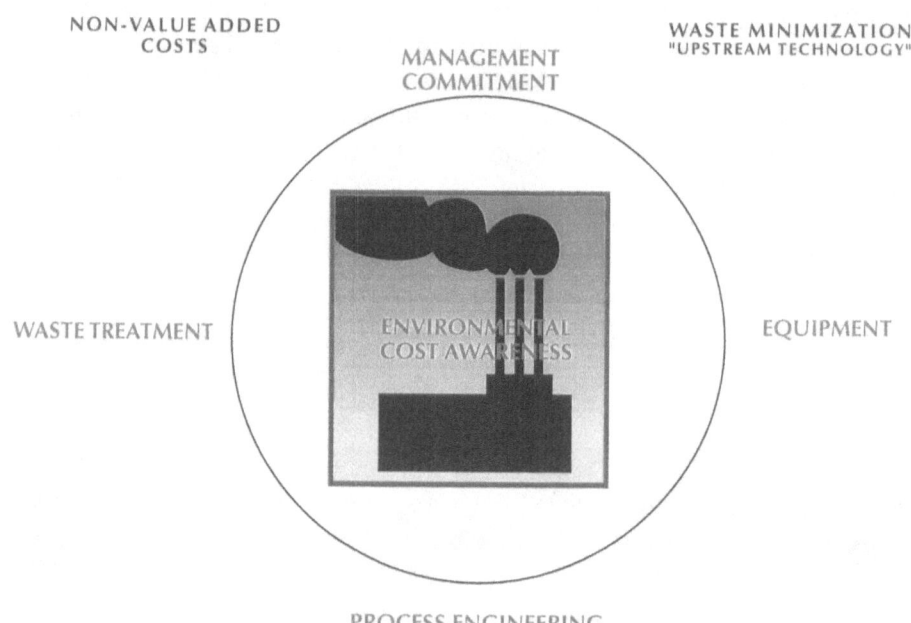

NON-VALUE ADDED
COSTS

MANAGEMENT
COMMITMENT

WASTE MINIMIZATION
"UPSTREAM TECHNOLOGY"

WASTE TREATMENT

ENVIRONMENTAL
COST AWARENESS

EQUIPMENT

PROCESS ENGINEERING

MATERIAL EFFICIENCIES

BUILD TO ORDER
SHIP DIRECT

THE COMPETITIVE EDGE

Joseph J. McHugh

Efficiency Factor #4
ENVIRONMENT

In this Chapter:
√ **Housekeeping and Safety**
√ **Waste Minimization**
√ **Engineering Support**
√ **Build-to-order**

In our journey toward competitiveness in the new millennium, attention to the ENVIRONMENT Efficiency Factor translates into profitability as well as social responsibility. Everyone shares an obligation for the maintenance of the environment, from waste generated in our personal lives to the engineering and production of life's needs. The latter stands as the largest generator of hazardous waste and places a significant burden on the environment. Consequently, we must all share in the protection of our earth, from engineering — especially if products are *manufacturing friendly* — to the final disposition of the finished product. If products are designed as *manufacturing friendly,* both the number of parts and amount of eco-waste are reduced.

HOUSEKEEPING AND SAFETY

Housekeeping and safety provide the foundation for a successful environmental program. Employee awareness and commitment to these important elements can promote significant material efficiency improvements, subsequently improving the ENVIRONMENT. Less clutter about the work place reduces equipment and product damage, as well as the reduction of spills, all of which generate waste.

Employees exercising good work habits can greatly improve material efficiencies. Material-yield improvements dramatically protect the environment. On the other hand, material rework clutters the internal environment. In essence, the achievement of maximum material efficiencies is a major step towards protecting our environment, be it landfills, atmospheric discharges, or industrial waste waters. The important concept is *waste minimization*.

WASTE MINIMIZATION

Product engineering and production personnel can provide a solid foundation for good environmental practices. Unfortunately, during the initial design, environmental considerations are often after-the-fact technologies. For example, a design engineer will without hesitation seek cost efficiencies for materials, machine, and manpower, but give only minimal attention to environmental costs. These costs are left to the manufacturer to manage as end-of-the-pipe technologies. After-the-fact methods of treating waste are expensive non-value-added costs, and as such, can no longer be accepted because of pressures from the increasing competitiveness of a global economy. To improve this efficiency factor, I encourage a commitment to *waste minimization*. *Waste minimization* starts with the materials and equipment suppliers and the processing engineer. The latter holds the keys to success in driving down the non-value-added costs associated with processing waste. In essence, you should look upstream to eliminate or limit hazardous discharges. In today's competitive environment, it is imperative for process and equipment engineering staffs to identify up front the various waste discharges to the atmosphere, waste streams, and landfills. In achieving this change in philosophy, the use of hazardous chemicals is of paramount concern.

Hazardous chemicals, or for that matter, *all* chemicals are detrimental to the environment. The subsequent handling of this waste by waste-treatment employees runs up non-value-added costs. Waste treatment facilities are a ripe area for helping to improve profitability. As managers, you should embark on a journey of better understanding this forgotten part of your business. Too often this costly department and its dedicated employees go without significant management attention. My experiences suggest that once you demonstrate an interest, your employees will offer ways to reduce this significant non-value-added cost. They know when excessive waste is discharged. They know when processing mistakes occur. They know the treating materials used and how programs may be implemented to help them achieve higher efficiencies. You should, therefore, solicit the knowledge of these responsible employees and grant them **freedom of professional expression.**

To achieve excellent chemical management, encourage process engineers, working with the materials suppliers, to redesign numerous chemical processes. A priority for the redesign of these processes is maximum utilization of limited resources, such as water, and limiting sewerage discharges to over-taxed waste-treatment facilities. In some cases, management will approve an expansion of waste- treatment facilities when we should be encouraging a reduction of waste *upstream* at the respective processes.

| Look Upstream |

We, as responsible managers of our company's and our earth's resources, simply do not have the liberty to cast upon society processing and chemical inefficiencies that we can control. Simply stated, end-of-the-pipe processing of waste won't cut it. Waste discharges must be drastically reduced, and the avenue to this reduction is process engineering working in harmony with materials and equipment suppliers.

The first line of defense against the introduction of potentially hazardous chemicals is the purchasing department. Too often chemicals are introduced without proper consideration for regulatory limits imposed on the hazardous discharges by governmental agencies. First and foremost, purchasing must assure the user of proper legal registrations, e.g., MSDS, TSCA, and so on. We must remember that the burden of responsibility rests with the user. Therefore, suppliers must be encouraged to take back any unused test chemicals. They must commit to just-in-time deliveries, thereby reducing plant site risks to employees and community.

Another important consideration is the lengthy liability associated with the generation and disposal of hazardous sludge. With each day the cost of disposal continues to escalate, thereby adding to more and more non-competitiveness in the global economy. Asian competitors are not burdened with these escalating environmental costs. Also the maintenance of sludge records, as imposed by regulating agencies, requires management to maintain a 30-year record of discharge manifests. This is a very expensive administrative expense. You should readily see the tremendous profit return you can have by drastically reducing waste *upstream,* at the source of discharge. By so doing, you can reduce non-value-added costs from point-of-discharge, to treatment, to disposal, to administration. What an opportunity!

As an Efficiency Factor guideline for managers, you should immediately commence data gathering of these negative costs by summarizing ENVIRONMENT expenses per unit-of-output. Having captured this cost, you can engage the cooperation of the respective parties to begin a dynamic program of setting monthly targets for the reduction of all wastes.

BUILD-TO-ORDER

Another avenue to reduce environmental costs is to *build-to-order* and ship direct. By implementing such a program, you can eliminate the hidden costs associated with mass production. Mass production creates inventory problems that generate waste through poor handling, obsolete products and so on. By building to order and shipping directly, damaged or obsolete goods will no longer be discharged to the environment. The challenge is identifying the intangible costs involved because many times finished goods pass to different departments and the subsequent cost of disposal is lost. A vivid example of this would be goods that fail under warranty and are subsequently returned for either repair or disposal. As many would say, "It's cheaper to throw away than repair." But the bottom line is negative environmental cost.

Today, we debate the challenges of the regulatory agencies because some argue that the costs do not justify the reduction of environmental wastes. I have a different view. **Environmental regulations *save* you money; they do not cost you money.** My experiences have justified this position, especially as related to ADVANCING TECHNOLOGIES, Efficiency Factor # 6.

CONCLUSION

In our journey toward *The Competitive Edge*, we have explored the Efficiency Factors of HUMAN RESOURCES, MATERIALS, EQUIPMENT, and the ENVIRONMENT. As we continue our adventure to global competitiveness, I will advance more dynamic, new ideas for continuous improvements. But before we explore the Efficiency Factors of ADVANCING TECHNOLOGIES, NON-VALUE-ADDED COSTS, and MANUFACTURING COSTS, let's pause at a cool oasis to reflect on some of the possibilities of OUTSOURCING.

OUTSOURCING
EFFICIENCY FACTOR #5

EDUCATIONAL
RE-DIRECTION

STRATEGIC PARTNERS

INTEGRATED
MANUFACTURING

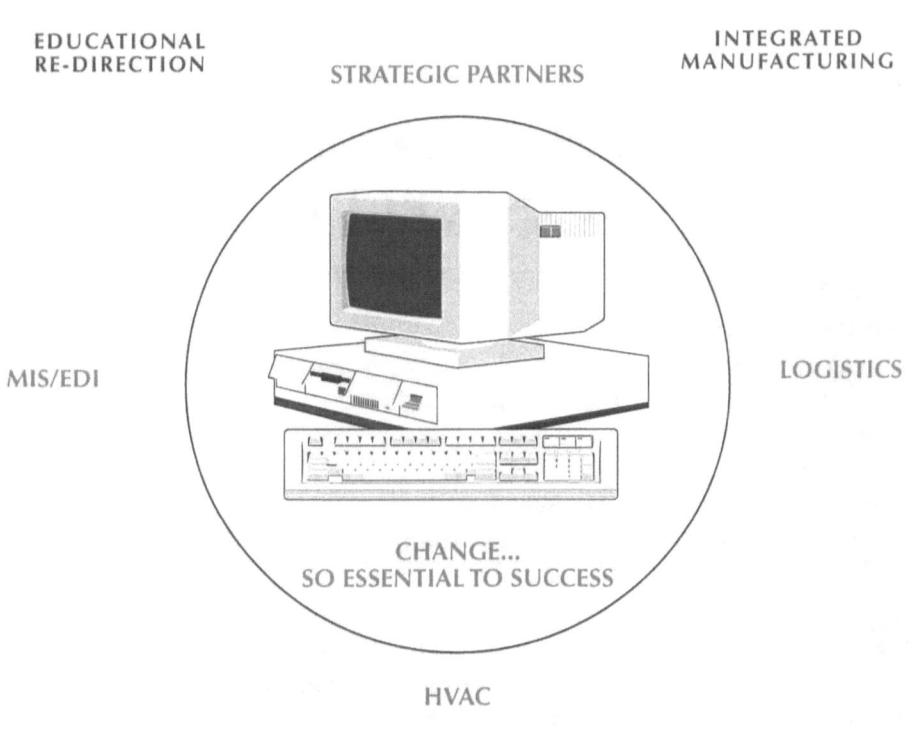

MIS/EDI

LOGISTICS

CHANGE...
SO ESSENTIAL TO SUCCESS

HVAC

CONSULTANTS VS.
HIRED MANAGERS

SHIP DIRECT

THE COMPETITIVE EDGE

Joseph J. McHugh

Efficiency Factor #5
OUTSOURCING

In this Chapter:
√ **Strategic Partnerships**
√ **Turnkey Systems**
√ **Incoming and Source Inspection**
√ **Warranty Failures**
√ **Logistics**
√ **Management Information Systems**
√ **Heating, Ventilation, and Air Conditioning**

While we rest from our journey under refreshing palm trees, let's explore the numerous opportunities offered by OUTSOURCING—seeking continuous improvements with specialists. This Efficiency Factor provokes the question: What is our core business? Today, too many organizations wrongly believe that they can master all activities within their organizations. Efficient organizations, however, continue to fine tune their core activities and outsource activities not in line with their main thrust for global competitiveness. OUTSOURCING offers fertile territory for savings.

For example, should an assembly company's resources be committed to the maximization of the assembly lines, or should these same resources be diluted by tracking raw materials and subsequently delivering the finished product? Why do so many companies employ expediters to track the delivery of component parts? I believe it is due to a lack of trust between the supplier and user. As I have stated many times, we must develop strategic partnerships by placing the burden of on-time deliveries squarely where it belongs, on the supplier. The material supplier should deliver the materials as needed even to the extent of maintaining limited inventories at *their* facilities.

Let's consider for a moment the delivery of chemicals used in production. The question here is should the end user stockpile inventory, in some cases, dangerous chemicals or should the local chemical supplier provide daily "milk runs"? Milk runs are a delivery procedure by which the chemical supplier will deliver daily those chemicals needed to | *Encourage Milk Runs* | support that day's production. This supplier does not have to be contacted daily by the user; instead, the supplier when delivering the various chemicals, checks the existing inventory and replenishes the chemical stock as necessary. By implementing this procedure, imagine the increased safety of employees, property, and community by the user limiting the level of dangerous chemicals. I encourage you as managers to seriously review your present procedures and see if a better, more efficient way of handling these materials might reduce non-value-added costs. Just ask the employees who handle these materials; they can offer some significant ideas about the elimination of redundant activities between the supplier and user. Some chemical suppliers will even offer to inventory, at their location, the chemicals they do not sell directly to the user. At any rate, chemicals provide only one example; other materials can similarly offer further cost improvements.

This change—and remember that **change is so essential to success**—is truly a cultural change that many are not willing to accept. But given time, global competition will force changes in this area.

Management must get involved in recognizing inter-company engineering and managerial limitations. Organizations that try to be a jack-of-all-trades and master-of-none will not survive. The trite saying, "we understand our business better than anyone," will not hold up because the Asian community is already committed to OUTSOURCING far greater than we can imagine. Let's continue to explore additional options for OUTSOURCING leading to further avenues of profitability: *turnkey systems* (noted in a previous Efficiency Factor), *incoming and source inspections, warranty failures, sub-assembly of small parts, logistics, MIS, EDI, and HVAC,* and finally *government.*

TURNKEY SYSTEMS

New or modified equipment purchases should be contracted under a *turnkey* arrangement. Here the equipment manufacturer has the sole responsibility of installing the equipment according to pre-determined parameters, as I presented in Efficiency Factor # 4: EQUIPMENT. This is truly an OUTSOURCING of responsibilities to the people who know the equipment the best, the equipment supplier. Furthermore, I propose that if several equipment suppliers are involved in the same project, one supplier should be contracted as the general contractor to prevent misunderstandings surfacing during the installation phase. When American-based companies purchase equipment from off shore, technicians from that company should be held accountable for its installation. The off-shore technicians should work in harmony with the user's line technicians or maintenance personnel to transfer the knowledge of the new equipment. Management must recognize the discontinuity and non-value-added costs associated with the supplier building the equipment and the user doing the installation. Many times these costs are looked upon as a necessary cost of increasing the capacity of the facility. In reality though, these costs continue to escalate, thereby driving the unit-cost higher than the competition. Certainly anyone advocating this type of management change would be pressed to support this position. I would offer, simply study the high costs of your equipment, engineering, and maintenance costs to ascertain whether or not this is a viable option. I'm betting yes.

INCOMING AND SOURCE INSPECTIONS

Incoming and source inspections offer another area for OUTSOURCING consideration. Why do many companies have incoming inspections? I would suggest that they maintain incoming inspections because they distrust their suppliers and fear shutting down the assembly lines. Source inspections—the sending of the user's employees to ascertain the supplier's compliance with specifications of the finished product—are also predicated on distrust. I disagree with both of these non-value-added expenses. *Incoming and source inspection* expenses are the sole responsibility of the supplier, and must be challenged by the user. This is truly a concrete avenue for OUTSOURCING, giving back to the supplier expenses where they truly belong. More and more companies today are doing just that. Managers cannot continue to accept the burden of costs to determine suppliers' compliance with specifications. Move immediately to curtail this cost.

As we continue to bask at this cool oasis, let's consider for a moment, divisions within the same company making component parts for each other. The user should not accept these inspection costs. Unfortunately, because the various operating units are within the same company, many do lip service and fail to take necessary actions to place the burden of these costs truly where they belong, on the supplier. As a manager, you should request a complete cost analysis of the non-competitive way you are presently doing business within your own organizations, especially with regard to the material movement expense.

WARRANTY FAILURES

Warranty failures are another area ripe for change. Today, all companies have warranty failures because we obviously do not live in a perfect world. However, you must ascertain the true annual cost of *warranty failures* including administrative and logistics costs. As is true in most cases, warranty failure costs should be the direct responsibility of the supplier, even within the same organization. Many companies have separate divisions to handle customer returns. These separate divisional expenses must be charged to the division who completed the final assembly. For the most part, however, major businesses transfer these costs to the corporate level. By doing so, the operating units are aware of the field failures but are not financially responsible. This is changing, but the change is slow in coming. Here is an opportunity to assess the viability of outsourcing the warranty-repair function because in-house efficiencies within a company do not justify maintaining this function. Analyze the advantages and disadvantages of performing *warranty failures* within. This opportunity presents an excellent case for analyzing whether you should outsource or not. An outside company chartered to do repairs and final disposition—and that's all they do, without the influence of a major company—can become extremely efficient and reduce costs for everyone. All costs associated with the OUTSOURCING of *warranty failures* will be the responsibility of the company's final assembler.

LOGISTICS

Another important area for you to consider OUTSOURCING is *logistics. Logistics* include the handling of raw materials and finished goods and the warehousing and shipment of the finished goods. Today, start-up logistics companies offer their services to help local companies reduce these tremendous non-value-added costs. But it many take a changing attitude on your part to test uncharted waters. Today, management should know the costs of tractor and trailer-rental expense, plus mileage, coupled with massive inventory spaces. I encourage you to test the waters by committing some percentage of your *logistics* needs to third parties and subsequently weighing the cost effectiveness of OUTSOURCING.

Here again, logistics suppliers can be more efficient because that is the only thing they do. Many of these suppliers have immediate access to trucking fleets, warehouse space shared by other companies, and experienced management. Moreover, they are committed and capable of handling the packaging of the finished product, the delivery to the end user, and the subsequent return of warranty failures. A company having its own logistics department can and many do demonstrate good efficiencies and sound management. The problem is the interaction between respective divisions within the company. Most intercompany divisions are assessed the costs of the logistics division; however, the operating units are focused on what they do best, assemble the finished product.

Should a company decide not to outsource logistics, they do have an alternative to reduce those costs by implementing *integrated manufacturing* and *shipping direct*. The first will require engineering know-how to balance the productive capabilities of the assemble line. Or as stated earlier, consider the *cell method of assembly*. This method would be the least expensive to implement. Which ever way you desire to go, both will provide significant opportunities to reduce *logistics* expenses.

MIS AND EDI

Within the administrative functions of any major company, one can find the acronym *MIS (Management Information Systems)* and *EDI (Electronic Data Interchange.)* *MIS* is very important administrative tool, providing the necessary information to monitor and improve profitability. Following the installation of an MIS system, employees are hired to maintain its functionality. My concern here is who provides the continual know-how about implementing the advancing technology and program changes happening each day. How can a growing company continue to introduce more efficient and faster information technologies? Today many companies who believe they can continue to upgrade MIS systems from within are making a grave mistake because their MIS staff lacks the time necessary to monitor the exploding information age and subsequently offer changes to management. I would guess at least 80 percent of a company's MIS staff is committed to maintaining the present system (hardware and software). Consequently, I truly believe that this is a fertile area for immediate OUTSOURCING. Companies should align themselves with efficient, proven software companies, as well as system-design companies, to help them maintain a high level of MIS services given the rapid growth of the information industry. Included in this information industry is *EDI*.

Electronic Data Interchange produces the capability to electronically transfer information at speeds beyond our wildest imagination. Today the service industry has leapfrogged industry by implementing accountability programs similar to EDI. Industry must pick up the charge by eliminating the antiquated administrative methods in place today. For example the purchase order, as I have said before, should be replaced by the efficient introduction of EDI. EDI can handle all transactions from issuance of purchase orders to the shipment of the user's finished product. All management has to do is simply say "do it now" and commit to this change to OUTSOURCING. Again the MIS department simply does not have the time to take on major changes such as this. People specialized in the field of EDI can implement and maintain this administrative change quickly and effectively. To support these positions, you should question the costs of issuing a purchase order, a payment check, and so forth. Companies with global growth in mind simply cannot wait to improve the information highway within their own organizations. Time is not in your favor, especially in the ever-expanding global economy. Next, as the cool breezes blow over us, let's consider another acronym: *HVAC*.

HVAC

Heating, ventilation, and air conditioning is another fertile area for OUTSOURCING consideration. More and more small companies cannot afford a maintenance staff to handle this responsibility, so they seek OUTSOURCING. Major companies should also study the cost effectiveness of OUTSOURCING HVAC, especially with regard to new facilities. Today some major companies provide efficient HVAC services twenty-four hours a day, seven days a week. They are committed to preventative maintenance, including parts inventory, as well as major repairs and equipment replacement. Without being redundant, I will simply propose that you commence a study of the effectiveness of OUTSOURCING what truly can become ever-increasing HVAC costs in the future.

GOVERNMENT

My final thoughts on this subject of OUTSOURCING are directed to the position of government. Today, as mot federal, state, and local governments struggle to find ways to reduce operating expenses and subsequently taxes, they must consider OUTSOURCING more and more or their responsibilities. Private, profit-motivated outsourcing companies have the expertise necessary to bring down the governmental costs of administering to the tremendous needs of some 261,000,000 Americans.

Included in OUTSOURCING is the very important area of management. Governmental agencies should be contracting proven managerial talent to assist in the merging of departments, the elimination of antiquated administrative practices, and the implementation of productivity measures. Elected officials, I believe, are considering this very approach. Fear of political upheaval by peers and subordinates is the negating factor. However with time, these barriers will be overcome because the new generation of politicians accepting political office has less fear of change. So as a parting shot at the concept of OUTSOURCING, government also should commit to cost-effective ways of running their various areas of responsibilities.

First, I propose that governments hire proven managerial talent, talent that will encourage productivity changes similar to business initiatives. The reason for hiring managerial talent and giving them the charter to implement cost-effective programs is because of the lessons we learned form the Grace Commission. The Grace Commission spent $75 million dollars to prepare and submit cost-effective programs to various governmental representatives. Not one of the recommendations was implemented. Consulting, in this case, did not work. Having outside management people with the authority to implement changes **will** work. Thereafter commence a program of OUTSOURCING, starting with the least desirable work and continuing to the major departures from the old way of doing things. This new awareness for efficient government will not readily be accepted. However, time has come to move governmental agencies to higher levels of efficiencies and OUTSOURCING is the avenue.

ADVANCING TECHNOLOGIES
EFFICIENCY FACTOR #6

DO IT NOW

MANAGEMENT
VIEW

TRAINING

GLOBAL
COMPETITION

GLOBAL
COMPETITION

THE FUTURE
IS TOMORROW

CONTINUOUS IMPROVEMENTS

EMPLOYEE
SKILL ASSESSMENT

CHANGE

PASSION TO INNOVATE
WITHOUT FEAR OF FAILURE

THE COMPETITIVE EDGE

Joseph J. McHugh

Efficiency Factor #6
ADVANCING TECHNOLOGIES

In this Chapter:
√ **Employment Matrix**
√ **Continuous Improvements**
√ **Do-It-Now**

A s we resume our travels towards competitiveness, let's pull out a telescope to see what's ahead: ADVANCING TECHNOLOGIES.

Today and tomorrow's advancing technologies are more demanding of business, education, and governmental organizations than ever before. As a matter of fact, if leaders from all sectors fail to comprehend the demands of this important Efficiency Factor, they simply are doing a disservice to their respective organizations and fellow employees. Technology levels in all industries are advancing so rapidly, they may even exceed the comprehensive level of your present staff. Numerous fields of ADVANCING TECHNOLOGIES are here today. Consequently, leaders of various organizations must commit to upgrading the skills of today's employees, while providing knowledgeable employees for the future. Leaders must assess today's employee skills, as well as provide the skills to manage the advancing technologies of the immediate future.

To maintain the technical skills of today's employees, as well as new employees, you should consider the annual *employment matrix* defined under the HUMAN RESOURCES Efficiency Factor. By implementing this matrix and updating it each month, you can get a handle on the demanding technology needs of the future. For example, suppose your organization plans to install new equipment or significantly modify your present equipment next year. If this is a commitment by management, then you should request, from the operating unit and the human resources department, the availability of the level of technical employees required. It simply is too late to purchase advancing technological equipment without the assurance of the technical staff to maintain it. Similarly, under the employment matrix or for that matter, a training matrix, the operating units should ensure the company management that technical training for the present staff will be implemented, lest they be left to sink or swim in the sea of ADVANCING TECHNOLOGIES.

As stated in EQUIPMENT Efficiency Factor, management should be encouraging *push-button technology*. You may recall that push-button technology implements computer-driven technology to provide line employees with the capability and transparent technology to change parameter settings at work stations. With push-button capabilities, model change can be made without expensive technical support from non-value-added departments, staff functions. Or as stated earlier, *integrated manufacturing* coupled with *manufacturing friendly products* (truly advanced technology given today's antiquated means of changing line configurations each time new models are introduced) is the best and most advanced way to go.

Here again with the challenges of a changing world, management must weigh the financial investment required versus the life of the advanced product design. This is why, I believe, Asian companies are deeply involved in the *cell concept of assembly*. The cell concept, as stated earlier, provides opportunities for line employees to do more assembly tasks than permitted by conveyor applications. Under the cell

| *Challenges of a Changing World* |

concept, one employee may very well assemble the complete finished product and even subsequently test it. This method, if applicable to your assembly technology, helps to limit capital investment, reduces idle time and maintenance costs, and truly provides for integrated manufacturing. My proposal here is for companies involved in assembly operations to set up a test station, say in a warehouse and try it. You just might be pleasantly surprised. I truly do not believe businesses have a choice. I believe you must continue to seek more efficient avenues to further reduce costs, and **continuous improvements** are the way to go.

Continuous improvements provide the absolute road map to success. You may recall that I commented on this earlier. Nevertheless it's worthy of repeating. Unless your organization demonstrates a continuing path of **continuous improvements,** your *competition* will achieve the competitive edge and gain increasing market share. For example, within the communications industry, hardware and software is advancing to new levels almost every nine to twelve months. Here is the most significant challenge to management especially with regard to the purchase of hardware. Today the Acer company of Asia has a ten-month plan: three months to design advancing technologies, six months to build, one month to eliminate inventories, and the cycle repeats itself. This is what companies in America must consider as they continue to find acceptable, competitive speeds on the information highway. The way to go is the plan I call *Do-It-Now*, as stated earlier. I won't go into detail here; I just want to emphasize the importance of this idea. If we continue to talk and talk without testing the implementation phase, we will always be playing catch up. If employees in your organization have a better idea, they should have the **freedom of professional expression,** and be permitted to implement the change simply by gaining peer acceptance and being able to professionally justify their position. For example, if you see better efficiency in changing equipment about the assembly line, you should *Do It Now.* Certainly some ideas won't work out, but I'm betting the number of successes under the plan will exceed the failures.

ADVANCING TECHNOLOGIES are the cornerstone of tomorrow. Unless we pursue better more efficient quality ways of doing our jobs, we will eventually fail in the long run. We cannot sit passively by while our competition is engineering better processes and products. With the past behind us, we must perform efficiently with a commitment to the present, recognizing the future is the key to our continued success. Each of us must be committed to generating new ideas to improve productivity, quality, and a continuous reduction of our costs, from issuance of purchase orders to shipment of the finished product. Each and everyday our minds are encouraging us to seek new ways of achieving and exceeding our goals. You must grab hold of the innovative ideas, share them with all, and as a team sort through and select the best for the new millennium. Then and only then will you be in a position to encourage new engineering, technology, and production of the highest quality at competitive costs.

As I have stated many times, ADVANCING TECHNOLOGIES must be coupled with *manufacturing friendly products* so that the labor content is so small, that companies can assemble the finished goods within the markets they serve. The vast knowledge of advancing technologies, coupled with the drive and determination of committed employees, will demand the managerial companion of wisdom.

We need the passion to innovate without the fear of failure.

Believing this telescope-view to the future will encourage a closer managerial look at ADVANCING TECHNOLOGIES, we can move to the next exciting leg on our journey to profitability with a most significant Efficiency Factor, NON-VALUE-ADDED COSTS.

NON-VALUE-ADDED COSTS
EFFICIENCY FACTOR #7

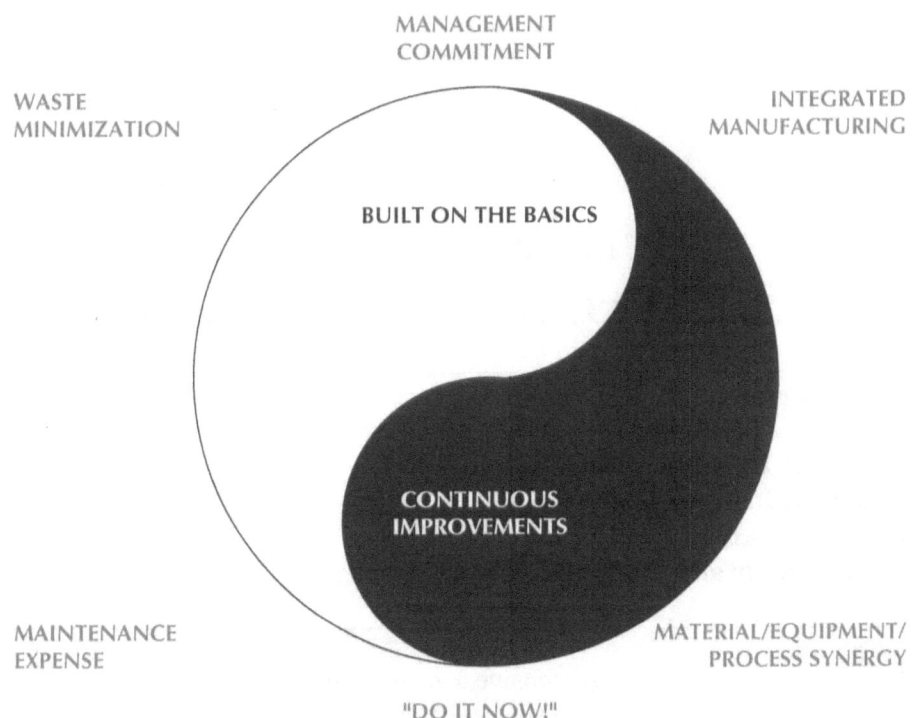

MANAGEMENT
COMMITMENT

WASTE
MINIMIZATION

INTEGRATED
MANUFACTURING

BUILT ON THE BASICS

**CONTINUOUS
IMPROVEMENTS**

MAINTENANCE
EXPENSE

MATERIAL/EQUIPMENT/
PROCESS SYNERGY

"DO IT NOW!"

ELECTRONIC DATA
INTERCHANGE (EDI)

PRODUCTIVITY, THE UNIVERAL
AVENUE TO SUCCESS

LOGISTICS "LOWER THE
WATER LEVEL" THEORY

THE COMPETITIVE EDGE

Joseph J. McHugh

Efficiency Factor #7
NON-VALUE-ADDED COSTS

In this Chapter:
√ **Production Schedules**
√ **Electronic Data Interchange**
√ **Handling, Delivery, and Storage**
√ **Production Areas**
√ **Cell Assembly and Integrated Manufacturing**

This Efficiency Factor is so extensive and such a major part of our journey that I will only touch the major contributors that undermine profitability. Much of the subject matter is covered under other Efficiency Factors. Here I bring it all together to assist you, as company leaders, in your drive for continuous improvements. This Efficiency Factor encompasses all the costs from issuance of purchase orders to receipt of materials, to all support functions, to environmental expenses, to warehousing and shipment of the final product. In essence, organizations should activate continuing programs to reduce NON-VALUE-ADDED COSTS by eliminating or reducing *everything* not adding value to the finished product.

Whenever materials or finished goods sit idle, money is lost. In the education arena, any time students have less than desirable grades, or the mix of disciplines is less than satisfactory, (e.g., too many business majors, too few engineering majors), society loses. When government agencies fail to measure productivity improvements across the board, business, education, and society loses. We need managerial commitment in all departments, in all organizations because inefficiencies in any one of numerous areas add costs to all others. We must be more demanding in defining and identifying NON-VALUE-ADDED COSTS and drive the wheels of efficiency to eliminate non-productive activities.

Today organizations spend huge sums to increase value-added efficiencies, such as advancing technologies, to gain greater productivity in areas like direct labor. Unfortunately, NON-VALUE-ADDED COSTS continue to linger or increase. Consequently, you must define these costs and encourage people who administer them to seek more efficient avenues of non-value cost cutting.

To begin this exciting leg of our journey, let's travel an imaginary road from issuance of purchase order to shipment of the finished product, with minor detours to environmental and maintenance expenses. During this part of our excursion, I will frequently pause to offer guidance about the best ways of reducing non-value costs.

PRODUCTION SCHEDULES AND "BLANKET" PURCHASE ORDERS

Our trek begins with the purchase order's issuance, followed by its acknowledgement and revision. Here I propose a paradigm shift that entails the user and supplier working in harmony—in a partnership arrangement. This positive change involves getting a commitment from the accounting department to replace the traditional purchase order with the *production schedule,* or at the least, the issuance of a *"blanket" purchase order.*

Using a *production schedule* instead of a purchase order offers advantages of cutting costs, as well as building a strategic partnership with the supplier. Each day the supplier is kept aware of the production level, for he has the sole responsibility to deliver materials to the user as needed. If the production output increases or decreases from the initial schedule, the supplier should adjust his deliveries accordingly.

Unfortunately, those who lack first-hand knowledge of this program's efficiency may balk at making changes. In that case the user should at least eliminate the redundancy of issuing numerous purchase orders for the same material, and move in the direction of issuing an annual *"blanket" purchase order.* This simplified approach will reduce some of the non-value-added administrative expenses.

Following the receipt of the materials, invoices are received, acknowledged, forwarded to accounts payable, and approved for payment. Here, as stated earlier, you could implement "self billing." Self billing is an administrative change through which the user acknowledges the receipt of materials as they come in and then transfers the information to accounting for payment. Here you eliminate the suppliers' need to issue invoices. Granted, this self-billing method is a significant change from daily practices. But significant changes like these are necessary to stay competitive in our expanding, global economy. This is just one example of the administrative efficiencies available to you. There is, however, a more advanced technology available out there on the information highway: *Electronic Data Interchange.*

EDI: ELECTRONIC DATA INTERCHANGE

From an operating point of view, I would like to simplify the procurement process. If you eliminate the redundancy of purchases orders, acknowledgements, changes, change acknowledgments, advanced-ship notices, receivers and receipt of same, followed by invoices, you will achieve unheard of efficiency improvements. I propose that all of the above be completely administered electronically by a study of, commitment to, and implementation of *Electronic Data Interchange* (EDI). Because of the various functions involved in its implementation—operations, MIS, and finance—the highest levels of management must exercise their prerogative by encouraging everyone to become more active in this advancing technology.

Since most of our key resources are focused on the operational side of our businesses, EDI studies should be conducted by other organizational functions, with the cooperation of an outside firm with expertise in the implementation of EDI. This third party could evaluate, expedite, and implement this electronic system to drive down NON-VALUE-ADDED COSTS. As everyone knows, we invest significantly in advanced operational technologies. Perhaps the time is right to strategically invest in automating your support functions.

As I mentioned earlier, the service industry has leapfrogged operational activities by implementing advanced automated systems. This situation truly indicates a need for the *Do-It-Now* plan for **continuous improvements.** Remember, if you are administering the acquisition of materials today as you have in the past, it's a safe bet that you competition is in the fast lane. I fail to understand how anyone can do redundant tasks day-in and day-out without targets to eliminate NON-VALUE-ADDED COSTS. Here is an area ripe for change.

HANDLING, DELIVERY, AND STORAGE

In my vision of the future, production-planning departments will issue schedules and systems design staff will automatically communicate them to suppliers, who will subsequently make and deliver the materials as needed. The areas of *handling, delivery, and storage* offer tremendous opportunities for continuous improvements. Today, most materials are shipped at the user's expense. Consequently, the supplier has little or no interest in reducing transportation costs because of the sinful term FOB, meaning that freight-forwarding costs are the user's expense. Note that I used the word *sinful* because suppliers who don't have to worry about this user expense have little incentive to help in reducing this non-value-added cost. I again encourage users to work in harmony with suppliers to lower this ever-increasing cost drain. By building a strategic partnership, the supplier would shoulder more responsibility in helping to achieve efficiency in moving and storing materials.

Moving and storing materials is perhaps one of the most significant negative costs to an operating unit. To reduce this outlay, the synergy between the supplier and user must come into focus, whereby the supplier studies ways to deliver the materials "as needed." The competitive global economy simply will not permit this heavy financial burden of non-value added costs. Departures of materials from the supplier must be coordinated with the user to help reduce the logistics costs of handling, trailers, and warehousing.

To contain and avoid these destructive costs, suppliers must take ownership and responsibility for the materials from their point of manufacture to final usage. As I perceive the new materials wave of the future, the user will network with the supplier about the daily usage of redundant materials by issuing a *blanket purchase order* and supplying daily production figures to the supplier who in turn prepares materials for delivery as needed. Also, the seller must accept responsibility for filling the pipeline, as well as accepting costs associated with discontinuity of delivers. Moreover, the supplier must guarantee the quality of products to relieve the user from the necessity of *incoming or source inspections.*

Incoming and source inspections must be eliminated because of their negative financial impact on the user. Develop strategic agreements with the supplier about the quality of the materials; if not, these costs of inspection should be assigned to your supplier. Emphatically encourage everyone involved in this function to seek **continuous improvements**, from issuance of purchase order to final shipment of the finished product.

PRODUCTION AREAS

Having received the materials, we next move to continuous improvement opportunities primarily in the *production areas.*

Within the assembly areas, opportunities for savings are evident especially with regard to conveyor lengths, space, and the number of indirect personnel to support the direct workers. The costs of buying, maintaining, and modernizing conveyors creates a negative impact on profits. Therefore operational managers should encourage a reduction in conveyor purchases and modifications.

The first step would be to determine the length that is actually *needed* for the conveyor. Consider such questions as these: Can we maintain and even increase output, while at the same time reducing conveyor length? Is the index time between functional stations too long? Or should the stations be moved closer together for increased productivity? I encourage setting a target plan to reducing conveyor needs by 35 percent, or the flip side, increasing output by 35 percent while maintaining the present length. Determining the most efficient length for the conveyor complement can result in an increase for other activities. For example, if you consolidate the conveyor and supportive equipment, valuable space will shortly become available and other tangible expenses such as maintenance, environmental, and utility costs will also be significantly reduced.

Another avenue for reducing conveyors, would be the implementation of what I called earlier the *cell-concept of assembly*. Without going into detail, this concept simply allows employees to assemble more of the finished product without the continuing need for conveyors. You need to explore this idea because of the potential for significant non-value-added cost reductions of model changeover time, maintenance, and so on.

You may also recall my suggestion for you to consider implementing *integrated manufacturing*. This plan adds to the effectiveness of present equipment configurations and supports the *cell concept*. Under the cell concept, integrated manufacturing can be implemented almost immediately without paying indirect employees to change line parameters.

Implementing the *cell concept* also reduces maintenance and environmental expenses—all purely non-value-added expenses. Unless a company is careful, maintenance expenses will continue to escalate because the main focus of operations is units-of-output. Each new annual budget will show a rising increase in maintenance expenses, including the costs of repair and operating suppliers. The *cell concept* will greatly reduce these burdensome outlays if, in fact, it is appropriate to a given level of production. Maintenance expenses also increase environmental costs because of the necessity to discharge hazardous oils, greases, and what all, using non-value-added manpower.

If you as managers rise to the challenge of reducing these expenses, you can greatly enhance the profitability of your company.

When you consider production methods—be they conveyorized or cell systems—you must also review your resulting warehousing costs. You may recall that I have identified warehousing costs as true NON-VALUE-ADDED COSTS, and as such they should be dynamically challenged by management. Two avenues for reducing these costs are worthy of repeating here. The first was *integrated manufacturing,* and the other was *shipping direct.* Both provide a tremendous opportunity for increasing profits by eliminating the voluminous amount of inventory carried by many companies. Warehousing costs include rental expense, tractor, trailer and fork lifts, personnel, and utilities. When a company implements *integrated manufacturing* and *ships direct*, these costs drop significantly and greatly improve the bottom line with little or no capital investment.

CONCLUSION

I propose that management commence an immediate program to reduce not only the unwarranted cost of warehousing, but all logistics expenses. The graphic of the rock and water level on the opposite page shows the indirect benefit of reducing all inventories. When the water level drops, other challenges magically surface. By addressing these additional "under water" challenges, you will, in short run, become more efficient and profitable. The question is, will you "dive in" or will the status quo prevail? Unfortunately, the global economy will not permit the status quo. We must *Do It Now!*

To further drive down NON-VALUE-ADDED COSTS, you can encourage an increase in productivity without further capital expenditures. This action will have a directly proportional positive impact on driving down these costs per unit. I believe this should be your first order of the day: requesting productivity improvement targets for all functional departments from purchase order to shipment of final goods and services, including all the non-value-added support functions.

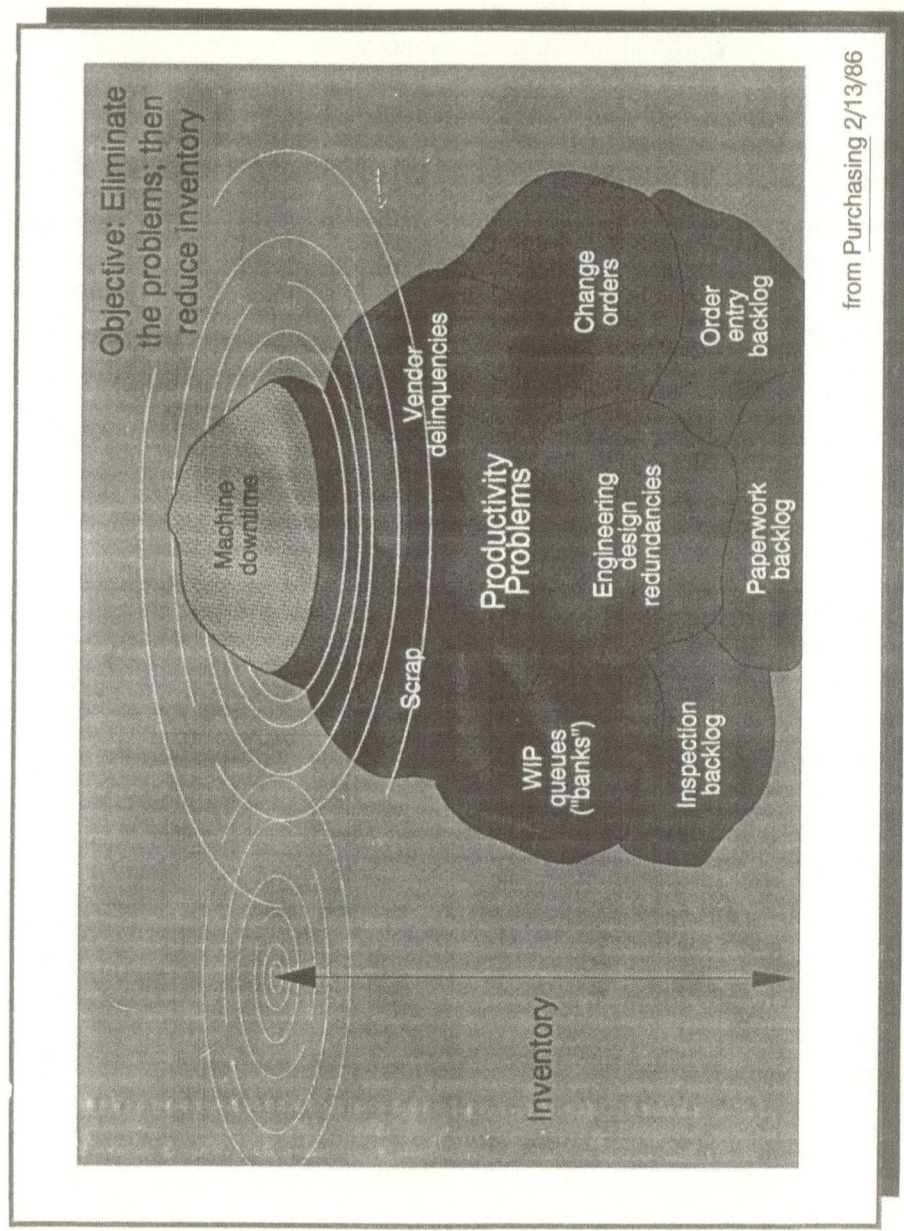

Finally, I would encourage you to consider all of these ideas whenever a decision is made to expand or start up a new facility. A new facility or expansion offers an opportunity to "do it right" the first time. It also offers a way to correct past mistakes and the opportunity to change the inefficiencies of the past. Remember, a commitment made during the start-up phase becomes difficult to alter later. It's better for management to over-extend itself in implementing ADVANCING TECHNOLOGIES and challenging employees to over-extend themselves and guard against excesses.

A new facility should enable employees to realize their true capabilities through **freedom of professional expression**, coupled with clearly defined targets. To assure maximum efficiency, proven professional managers should be employed to guide the expansion to more efficient methods of doing business, while at the same time guarding against excessive wastes of investment dollars. Simply assigning this responsibility to someone within the present organization won't cut it. Companies need professionals with no ties to the present function because long-standing business and social contacts dilute the effectiveness of management staff. Therefore, by employing an independent expert who has been through various expansions, your company can maximize productivity, profits, and **continuous improvements.**

To be competitive today, commit immediately to encouraging continuous improvements and drastic reductions of your NON-VALUE-ADDED COSTS. I have touched briefly on various areas of NON-VALUE-ADDED COSTS and how you can implement their reduction. Time is not in your favor because of the escalating demands of a global economy. Just because your company may be profitable now is no justification for resisting continuous improvements and shouldering excessive NON-VALUE-ADDED COSTS.

We must constantly assert ourselves; otherwise the profitability of today may not finance the inefficiency of tomorrow.

Given a reasonable profit level, you should set targets for continued earnings growth. An immediate reduction in NON-VALUE-ADDED COSTS, even without increased capital or sales, can offer a significant financial return. All of these money-saving reductions also have a direct influence on a concurrent drive to reduce MANUFACTURING COSTS, the next leg of our journey.

MANUFACTURING COSTS EFFICIENCY FACTOR #8

PRODUCTIVITY
MEASURE

MATERIAL SUPPLIER

MANAGEMENT
ENCOURAGEMENT

MAINTENANCE
EXPENSE

UNIT
COST

SPOILAGE

NON-VALUE ADDED COSTS

EMPLOYEE
COMMITMENT

HOUSEKEEPING

INTEGRATED MANUFACTURING

THE COMPETITIVE EDGE

Joseph J. McHugh

Efficiency Factor #8
MANUFACTURING COSTS

In this Chapter:
√ **Personnel Expense**
√ **Mainline Defects**
√ **Model Changeovers**
√ **Maintenance Expenses**
√ **Utility Costs**
√ **Housekeeping**

Nearing the end of our exciting voyage to competitiveness, we will explore the final Efficiency Factor, MANUFACTURING, which deals primarily with the costs of production and assembly operations. Even though the focus is business, many education and governmental organizations can glean ideas for continuing to improve the efficiency of their respective organizations.

Within this section I will guide you in searching for **continuous improvements** in production and assembly, setting improvement targets, and then measuring those productivity improvements. We will also take side trips to visit the associated costs of manufacturing such as maintenance, material handling, and so on. These expenses, you may recall, were also part of NON-VALUE-ADDED COSTS. Within the manufacturing operations, these costs become more significant because of the sheer size of the manufacturing budget.

PERSONNEL EXPENSE

Personnel, both direct and indirect, form the largest percentage of a manufacturing budget. Consequently, managers must analyze manufacturing costs to assure the efficiency of the personnel committed to this Efficiency Factor. The measures of productivity, units-of-output per employee and unit-cost, remain essential factors to determine the continuing profitability of any business.

Because personnel expenses represent the greatest percentage of MANUFACTURING COSTS, companies must create guided targets for continuous productivity improvements. As part of the management staff, you should measure this productivity by one of two means: units-of-output per employee (both direct and indirect) per year OR unit-cost per unit-of-output per year. These productivity measures must ascend; otherwise, the competitive nature of business will cause your company to remain stuck in "competitive catch-up mode." To avoid this situation, benchmark your productivity measures against whoever are your most effective and dynamic competitors. This means an addition to non-value-added costs; however, it is vital for your organization to know the competitive nature of its industry and the markets it serves.

Anytime manufacturing expands, you must be extremely careful about the number of additional employees requested by your operating units, especially with regard to indirect personnel. In fact, business expansions offer you as managers the opportunity to truly test the full capabilities of your employees. You may recall, earlier I suggested that many employees are capable of exceeding their output if managers would grant **freedom of professional expression**. Now I will go one step farther to suggest that **management personnel has no right to gauge the true capabilities of those reporting to them**, especially indirect personnel. The potential for individual growth and self-actualization is strengthened during periods of expansion. Also within a guideline I offered earlier was the idea that preceding the employment of additional employees, you should first test the true capabilities of your present staff; should additional employees still be warranted, hire a few, test their true capabilities and so on. I offer this guideline because it is so easy to hire employees and so difficult to reduce staff that should never have been hired in the first place. One generation of management staff may hire too many employees, only to leave the burdensome task of employee reduction to another generation.

With regard to the hiring of direct employees, you must similarly be careful because time studies may not support additional direct personnel. My guide here would be first to implement job consolidation before the employment of additional direct personnel. In other words, each direct position must be challenged about its necessity and possibly consolidated with other positions. Later I will comment on line speeds and how productivity may be improved without the employment of additional personnel. I will leave this *personnel expense* item for the moment, but suffice it to say that the costly employment of additional personnel must be well-documented and convincing to management. Here again the *employment matrix* provides an excellent tool for forecasting the continuing employment needs of your organization.

To be competitive throughout the markets any business serves, a company must continue to show **continuous improvements**, from issuance of the purchase order to the shipment of the final goods and services. Since the field of opportunities for continuing improvements is rich, here I will offer guidelines for further productivity improvements and the subsequent reduction of the all-important cost per unit-of-output. First, measures of productivity and costs must be suggested by management and accepted by the respective parties chartered with the responsibility for achieving them. My guideline here would be to set realistic but challenging targets. These targets should reach higher than the standard 10 percent used so many times. Let's review some of the many ways productivity can be improved.

MAINLINE DEFECTS

With regard to improving productivity (i.e., units-of-output per employee), managers should first challenge every means of improving productivity before committing to capital investments. For example, determine the percentage of *mainline defects*, and subsequently plan a meaningful, accountable, immediate program for the reduction of these. If an organization has multiple shifts, the second-shift personnel can also enhance this meaningful program. Mainline defects are costly in many ways; they diminish output and quality and add extensive non-value-added rework expense. Furthermore, *mainline defects* negatively impact spoilage, the true loss of valuable material resources. Spoilage reduces productivity and drives up non-value-added costs for disassembling to save expensive parts, work stations, maintenance, and the environmental discharge of both hazardous and non-hazardous materials. Finally, even administrative and logistics costs rise because of retrieving additional materials to provide for what is believed to be "normal spoilage" (I dislike that term) and spoilage higher than the expected norm. So setting meaningful targets to reduce this burdensome cost to management can have a positive financial impact. Next let's move to guidelines pertaining to *model changeover* time, line speeds, and throughput time.

MODEL CHANGEOVERS

Model changeover time presents special challenges for companies attempting to increase productivity and make sound financial decisions about investing in additional capital equipment. Often product designers give scant attention to the problems of the actual model changeover. Yet this limited thinking must give way to what I offered as *manufacturing friendly products.* If product designers are committed to this redirection, operations managers must challenge the length of time to change the assembly lines to new and different models. Let's look at a worst case. Suppose 50 employees are engaged in the assembly of products; a required model change causes down time for all employees, quite an expense to management. Instead, operations personnel must present clearly defined targets to minimize this changeover time, and, if possible, schedule program changeovers for non-working hours.

Another approach to reducing *model changeover* losses would be to produce similar models in tandem, provided the customer base will permit this. Remember two additional guidelines I presented earlier: First, plan and implement *push-button technology.* You may recall that *push-button technology* provides line operators with a computerized method of changing their work stations by simply pushing a button to change the parameter settings in line with customer expectations. Following an exhaustive study and the implementation of this advancing technology, I also suggest the plan of *integrated manufacturing. Integrated manufacturing* allows any one of many assembly lines to produce different models or different sizes integrated on the same assembly line. This plan demands a finance study of the cost of any additional equipment, versus the unit-cost. Customers' time expectations of the future and the reduction of logistics costs also need to be factored in. I believe that many companies will find no alternative to *integrated manufacturing* in the future because of the competitiveness of the global economy and the cost-efficiency demands of the customer as we move towards a new millennium.

An additional avenue to improving productivity would be an exhaustive study to shorten throughput time and increase line speeds. Shorter throughput time involves combining employee tasks; eliminating antiquated, lingering processes; and shortening distances between various stations.

Shorten Throughput Time

All of these will provide productivity improvements essential to increasing line speeds. Increasing these speeds must be the first order of business prior to committing to new capital investment. Many times seconds can be shaved off of adjustment stations, transit time, and redundant inspection stations, as well as the final packaging activities. Increasing line speeds can be implemented without any increase in employment. Certainly any one of a number of stations may be on the critical path; however, getting all parties together and implementing *Do-It-Now* can provide efficiencies well beyond the level predicted. Study and implementation will have a dynamic impact on the reduction of unit-cost.

Unit-cost is an important measure to be established prior to any commitment to produce goods and services. To truly define goods and service pricing, a company must know the unit-cost as well as the benchmark cost of one's competitor. Given the completion of this study and a decision to commit to the production of the goods and services, managers like you must continue to set targets for further reductions of unit-costs. Let's take a look at some of the costs in danger of getting out of control unless guiding targets are in place and monitored monthly.

MAINTENANCE EXPENSES

Maintenance expenses, including environmental costs, will continue to escalate unless management creates and guides programs necessary to curtail these. Often maintenance expenses are falsely believed to rise parallel with increasing production. This is simply not the case. All maintenance expenses, including the all-important preventative maintenance, must be monitored very carefully. This includes everything from employee needs—clothing, tools and so on—to oils, greases, spare parts, outside contractors, environmental support personnel, agency permits, waste hauling fees, taxes and so on. Suffice it say, maintenance costs are one of the greatest non-value-added costs to any organization. Service industries, as well as major manufacturers, face a continuous cost challenge in reducing heating, ventilation, and air conditioning costs. To assist maintenance departments in reducing their costs, operating units should reduce conveyor length. In fact, where possible, manufacturing should eliminate conveyors, especially electrical-driven ones, by replacing them with gravity feed conveyors; or for that matter, if the product is light enough, simply have employees manually move products to the next station. In my time I have observed conveyors serve simply what I call managerial "showmanship": the automation looks great to an outsider, but may actually be hindering the per unit-cost output. Moreover, many conveyorized systems are used for heating and cooling applications. As advancing technologies provide more efficient parts with longer life expectancy and fewer parts, the elimination of conveyors may reduce utility costs.

UTILITY COSTS

In most cases, *utility costs* are reviewed by the operating units. However, unless the product and service design people commit to becoming part of a team chartered to reduce utility expenses, operations staffs will be handicapped in reducing this cost. I suggest that you should contract this task to a third party because local managers are primarily committed to increasing productivity and reducing other more obvious unit-costs. Many may disagree with this strategy; I suggest that you request an internal audit, and then compare the results with financial savings offered by outsourcing to a third party.

PRODUCTION SUPPLIES

Production supplies offer yet another opportunity to reduce manufacturing costs. These supplies cover everything from employee needs to direct and indirect materials used on or about the assembly lines and by administrative staffs. My proposal here is for you to focus on every financial line entry associated with these supplies. For example, are various pastes or paints used in the manufacturing process? If so, sample the supplies daily in order to set limit guidelines about the amount used. Are tubular pastes being used where employees are cutting the openings too large? At any rate, without further detail, request a continuing decrease in this cost, especially for production supplies that are non-value-added.

HOUSEKEEPING

Another area for cost reductions is *housekeeping*. Effective housekeeping practices can help reduce costs by eliminating clutter around operating units. Clutter causes accidents to both employees (workers' compensation) and products. For example, material movement in some cases is extensive; lacking the space for its movement leads to damage of not only the component parts, but also the finished product. Thus, improving housekeeping offers numerous financial returns as well as improving the image of a company and its management. The outside appearance of buildings, offices, and operating units reflects the level of orderliness, quality, and professionalism that suppliers and customers will associate with the company. *Housekeeping* becomes a reflection of how management addresses the proficient needs of the business.

> *Appearances Do Matter*

LOGISTICS ARENA

My final thoughts for reducing MANUFACTURING COSTS lie in the *logistics arena*. I say *arena*, because this is truly an area for collective efforts by various departments to reduce costs significantly. Here I am talking about costs from shipment of raw materials, to movement of materials about the operating units, to shipment of waste, and finally to shipment of the finished goods. Logistics costs include personnel, rental of equipment and warehouses, and land space. This arena for cost reduction offers tremendous opportunities for companies because often these costs are allocations from various operating units, and as such, fail to get the complete attention of some management teams. If an organization is huge, with multiple facilities, chances are the company has a separate logistics division. If so, you must set targets to reduce this non-value-added cost per unit-of-output. You must seek more efficient methods of material management because the competitive edge of the future will go to those in position to ship finished goods directly from point of manufacture to the end user. Today, component parts are obtained from any number of sources, pulled together, and then shipped to the end user. Tomorrow's competition will be providing more material-handling efficiencies to the end user. The most effective material-handling operations will get the lion's share of the market.

Also, consider a change in operating procedures when it comes to the receipt of raw materials or component parts. For example, in most cases today, the purchasing division orders materials; coordinates with the various suppliers; and working through expediters, schedules the materials for shipment and receipt. The future will show this method to be obsolete and inefficient. My guideline allows that following issuance of a purchase order, (or better yet simply issuance of the production schedule), the responsibility for material movement and receipt rests with the logistics department. Too often materials arrive, to the surprise of some, only to be inventoried and stored for later use, creating non-value-added expense that only increases unit-cost. Should you have doubts as to the effectiveness of this proposed method of material movement, consider how supermarkets ship finished goods: daily food products are received as needed because of refrigeration and freshness requirements. Today people in Asian countries are developing this supermarket method of handling materials, as are some American-based companies. **These new procedures show why continuous improvements are a must, and change is so essential to success.**

CONCLUSION:

MANUFACTURING or OPERATING COSTS, depending on the function of your business, demand close monitoring and new target setting to improve productivity and reduce unit costs. Otherwise your business will simply not be competitive in the ever-increasing global economy. I encourage you to request an all-inclusive cost analysis of your current business practices and then set meaningful targets for its reduction. Within this Efficiency Factor I have offered numerous ways of improving your bottom line. Certainly all the roads to cost reduction are too numerous to be included in this short itinerary. Nevertheless, I trust I have generated interest in driving your business, educational, or governmental unit to realize the competitive challenges surfacing across the planet. The opportunities for improving profitability are enormous. All you have to do is ***Do It Now!***

Measurements of Management
X-MATRIX

With the outline of the Eight Efficiency Factors behind us, we now turn our exploration to methods of measurements for managers. The Introduction highlights some proposed methods of measurements. For purposes of this tour for managers, I will focus on the world-recognized X-MATRIX method.

X-MATRIX provides a highly effective way for coordinating, planning, monitoring, and measuring a business plan and the actions necessary to achieve clearly defined targets. First the president or operating committee approves the business plan and sets the boundaries and targets necessary to achieve higher levels of efficiency. Once they establish the company's broad objectives, the next level of management defines specific objectives in line with the approved direction of the organization. Next, as we get closer to the daily operations, those responsible for hands-on activities complete their objectives. Throughout the chain of preparing X-MATRIX, the president or operating committee's objectives are general in scope, while those chartered with more operating responsibilities further define the objectives, and finally the hands-on personnel must be very definitive about how best to implement and drive the operating unit's master plan.

To be successful, this effective method for measuring management objectives requires analytical and self-disciplinary skills of each individual. It further demands the direct support and monitoring of top management. Otherwise, I know from past experience, the X-MATRIX will | *A Scientific Method* | simply become "another program of the month." To drive the effectiveness of this scientific planning method, I encourage top management to incorporate X-MATRIX presentations into your monthly financial meetings. Experience has shown that when this is done, all responsible parties will recognize your interest and be more willing to commit the discipline necessary for continuing to implement and succeed financially with such a program. Therefore, before committing to X-MATRIX, you must be assured of the time

| A Proven Method |

and effort of your management team to support this scientific method of measurement. In some companies the monthly monitoring support may come from a small committee made up of members from finance, operations, and hands-on-employees (both direct and indirect personnel). Before moving on to the mechanics of X-MATRIX, I am reminded of the management model introduced many years ago, Management By Objectives (MBO). The X-MATRIX, in my professional opinion, is a further extension of MBO, but requiring monthly monitoring, unlike the quarterly monitoring of MBO. I would encourage you to seriously consider implementing X-MATRIX or some other model your organization is comfortable with. When you are asked about your progress in planning, implementing, coordinating, or monitoring a business plan, you can readily offer the X-MATRIX as a proven method of managing and monitoring your business.

The X-MATRIX measure (Appendix A) consists of four sections: *Objectives, Items, Targets, and Gain. Objectives* are determined first, and then *Items* are clearly defined to achieve the objectives. *Targets* are collectively agreed to, and *Gain* indicates the financial return of achieving the targets. As you list the *Objectives* on the left side of the "X", begin with those objectives offering the greatest return to the organization. Moving to the top of "X," you list the major contributing *Items*, to further define the path leading to the Targets. Under the *Items*, you will notice when listing them that some will have a positive influence on other *Objectives*, thereby realizing a gain greater than expected. Moving to the right of "X," you would list the *Targets* your team agrees to. Next to the *Targets,* the X-MATRIX chart is designed to identify responsible departments and individuals who claim each main responsibility or sub-responsibility. And finally on the right side of "X" are columns providing for a timetable, or what some may call "time milestone commitments." Moving to the bottom of "X" is *Gain*. Here the rewards of everyone's commitment come into focus. These itemize the cost reductions or profitability realized from the entire organization's effort, from top management to hands-on personnel. Finally as also defined by X-MATRIX, a series of dot patterns going from three corners of "X" show the numerous interactions of the *Objectives, Items, and Targets* all converging on **Gain**.

This then is a brief summary of one way to systematize your commitment and know-how into achieving a business plan. I would like to state one more time that X-MATRIX is as near to a science for monitoring management objectives as you will have the exciting opportunity to work with. Here again, the success of this method of measurement, as is true with others, demands support and monthly monitoring by top management. Hopefully I have stimulated the interest of those responsible for improving operations throughout business, educational and governmental organizations before moving on to the final section of this voyage: THE PLAN.

Do It Now!
THE PLAN

The Eight Efficiency Factors outlined on this pilgrimage to universal competitiveness provide numerous opportunities for business, educational, and governmental organizations to improve efficiencies. These efficiencies range from issuance of purchase orders to shipment of the final goods and services. Areas for efficiency also include the support functions that bill operating units for their services. These efficiency guidelines provide various avenues of opportunity for your company to travel, while at the same time encouraging detours because often productivity and cost improvements in one area lead to other opportunities. As stated earlier, you as managers must encourage **continuous improvements** because of ever-increasing global competition. Consequently, the success and completion of any objective becomes an opportunity to seek additional efficiencies so necessary to remain competitive.

The following outline of THE PLAN highlights several guidelines presented throughout the Eight Efficiency Factors. These guidelines will not go into detail, but rather will serve as a reminder about the value of each factor. I will also offer methods and charts for implementing THE PLAN including the measures as they exist today, the major objectives, targets, timelines, and measures. You may, on the other hand, elect to implement the Efficiency Factors by using your present systems for improvements. I would further propose that you seek financial gain greater than the standard 10 percent. Experience has shown me how successful an improvement team can be if given **freedom of professional expression.** Coupled with any improvement objective is the exposure of other opportunities, as well as intangible returns to be realized from your management's efforts and support.

Good luck on your journey to becoming a more exciting and competitive operation. And now THE PLAN:

First, establish a basis as to where your organization is today. This can be your most recent monthly financial statement, average units-of-output, or cost-per-unit. Productivity is measured by units-of-output per employee per year, or revenue per employee per year should be determined and will form the foundation for measuring improvements. Likewise, the average unit-cost, say for the past six months, will serve as an additional foundation for measuring improvements. Next, managers like you must set the general objectives, timetables for completion, and methods of measurement. Here I propose several ideas for guiding the success of innovative new programs.

> *Establish a Basis*

The first guideline is to consider forming a monitoring committee of three individuals: one from finance, a statistician, and, what I call, a "technocrat." A technocrat is an experienced product or procedural engineer with financial savvy to support the numerous product or systems design changes. Consider an outsider for the chairmanship of this committee, with the other three being employees of the organization. This plan proves superior to hiring a team of outside consultants who may set things in motion but lack responsibility and may leave your organization to stumble on its own after the consultants leave. An outside chairperson still guides from an objective perspective, but the small committee of three insiders provides continuity following the departure of the hired chairperson. These key points are worthy of repeating: an outsider, with the proper authority is, I believe, a must! The three key team members create a bridge of continuity necessary to support your ongoing improvement programs. The outsider, the chairperson, provides a new set of eyes, coupled with extensive experience to provide significant input and profitability far in excess of his or her fee. As I offered earlier, *Do It Now!*

Once top management has formulated the general objectives and time tables, lower levels of management become more definitive about implementing and achieving the objectives. To guide this activity, I offered the controlling program:X-MATRIX. Appendix A is a diagram for implementation of this exciting program. Remember, X-MATRIX is as near a science of implementing and controlling financial improvements as one can be exposed to. Yet X-MATRIX demands the support of management each month. Otherwise the program will lose its effectiveness within time. Should you have concerns about compliance with the monthly demands of this program, I offer some additional means of monitoring **continuous improvements.**

> *X-Matrix*

Starting with the executive committee, management can implement HLA. You may recall that High-Level Activities are a priority listing of everyone's commitment to **continuous improvements.** Each individual lists those areas of improvement that provide the most immediate and greatest return to the organization. Employees must weigh the amount of valuable time available for both the assigned daily tasks of their positions and their commitment to seek improvements.

Thermometer
Measure

Should HLA guidelines be suggested by management as a way to monitor ideas, implementation, and measures, every level of the organization should be so committed. And let's not forget the administrative employees because they are truly at the core of most activities. In support of HLA, I further propose the implementation of the *Do-It-Now* method of measuring continuous improvements. This method is simple to say the least; it is the very visible charting of successes by utilizing the often-forgotten thermometer. This method of measure should be color coded by improvement objectives and displayed throughout the various functional departments. The thermometer must also have a color assigned for each functional department so all can see the commitment and successes of each department.

Another method of monitoring the successes of the Eight Efficiency Factors is shown in Appendix B, the Efficiency Factors Control Chart. This method provides for listing *Objectives, Base Period figures, Targets, Action Items, Responsibility, and Time Line.* This is a very simplistic, yet effective way to monitor continuous improvements.

The final method for monitoring improvements is the Efficiency Factors Organizational Plan whereby teams are formed to implement and guide the improvement objectives. This method is lead by a committed chairperson, usually a member of the executive committee or the ranking officer. The teams are composed of the major functional department such as *Production, Quality, Design, Administrative Logistics, and Materials,* or other function names more in line with your organization. This organizational structure can be found in Appendix C.

These methods are valuable for implementing and monitoring the successes of the Eight Efficiency Factors. With objectives, targets, timelines, and measurement methods in mind, let us now revisit some of the highlights of each of the Efficiency Factors. The Eight Efficiency Factors as outlined in this book are, once again, HUMAN RESOURCES, MATERIALS, EQUIPMENT, ENVIRONMENT, ADVANCING TECHNOLOGIES, OUTSOURCING, NON-VALUE-ADDED COSTS AND MANUFACTURING COSTS.

HUMAN RESOURCES HIGHLIGHTS

- This efficiency factor is the guiding principle and the most expensive part of any functional budget.
- Continuous improvements are the theme of *The Competitive Edge,* and employees exercise and implement these changes.
- Freeze employment, consolidate positions, and reduce the number of titles and positions.
- Advancing technology demands continuous training.
- Provide for an annual employment matrix and rolling employment.
- Employment of temps may be a license to steal and may negate conceptual skills.
- Employee empowerment provides for freedom of professional expression. Nevertheless, management must be involved.

MATERIALS HIGHLIGHTS:

- Materials include both direct and indirect materials as well as maintenance repair and operating supplies. Collectively these represent the second highest cost to management.
- Supplier selection and the number of suppliers directly influence profitability.
- Strategic partnerships with suppliers are imperative to improve material yields, reduce environmental discharges, and assist in the reduction of non-value-added costs from issuance of purchase orders to shipment of finished goods and services.
- Provide synergistic support to the equipment supplier and processing engineer.

EQUIPMENT HIGHLIGHTS

- Total Equipment Productivity checks increasing present equipment output prior to the commitment of investment dollars. Challenge yields, downtime, line defects, and maximum speed capability.
- Return on Investment requires justification for present equipment modification and purchase of new equipment versus "nice to have."
- Implement the Green-Light method of equipment analysis.
- Test the capability of new equipment to meet the challenges of advancing technology.
- Technical staff must hold the qualifications to support advancing technology.
- Turnkey systems are a must!
- Push-button technology extends the technical know-how of line personnel.

- Product design should focus on manufacturing friendly products.
- Implement integrated manufacturing.
- Test the value of cell assembly.

ENVIRONMENT HIGHLIGHTS

- Commit to an exhaustive study of environmental costs per unit of output; it is all non-value-added expense.
- Encourage synergy between material and equipment suppliers and the all-important processing engineer.
- Define and set targets to reduce material waste throughout the business unit.
- End-of-the-pipe methods of handling waste won't cut it! The name of the game is *waste minimization.*
- Design products with environmental considerations in mind.
- Study and implement build-to-order and ship direct.
- Companies with multiple locations maintain one and the same environmental standard.

ADVANCING TECHNOLOGIES HIGHLIGHTS:

- Evaluate investments in advancing technology versus the life of the new technology.
- Weigh investment versus the always-present need for continuous improvements.
- Create employment and training matrixes for technical staff.
- Present staff must maintain technical competency to meet the challenges of advancing technology.
- Change is essential to success.
- Review push-button applications, integrated manufacturing techniques, and the cell-assembly concept.
- Finished goods should be assembled within the markets served.

OUTSOURCING HIGHLIGHTS:

- Employment of temps and janitorial services is outsourcing.
- Suppliers maintain inventory and deliver on time.
- Incoming and source inspections are pure outsourcing to suppliers.
- Logistics should be exhaustively studied.
- Equipment installation is outsourced by agreeing to turnkey systems.
- Warranty failures should be handled by the producing unit or a third party.

- Heating, ventilation, and air conditioning services should be considered for outsourcing, especially for new facilities.
- MIS/EDI: The information highway is changing so fast that in-house personnel simply do not have time for designing and implementing new programs efficiently.

NON-VALUE-ADDED COST HIGHLIGHTS:

- Challenge everything from issuance of purchase orders to shipment of finished goods and services.
- Maintenance and environmental costs provide significant opportunities.
- Purchase order versus a production schedule and self-invoicing offer opportunities for change.
- Freight-On-Board: what a sin!
- Electronic data interchange has become the efficient wave of the future.
- Build-to-order and ship-direct are musts in a global economy.
- Value added is imperative.

MANUFACTURING COST HIGHLIGHTS:

- Direct and indirect personnel costs are the highest budgetary expense.
- Material spoilage and associated environmental costs offer opportunities for profit improvements.
- Equipment efficiency is a contributing factor.
- Productivity and unit-cost measures expose non-value-added costs.
- Maintenance costs provide an avenue to profitability.
- Your focus must be on continuous improvements each and every day.
- Efficient space utilization offers significant opportunities. Are you sure you need additional space?
- Evaluate the cost of utilities and services per square foot of space.

You are finally at the end of your journey to *The Competitive Edge*. Before this treasure trove of valuable ideas slips away from you:

Do It Now!

APPENDIX A

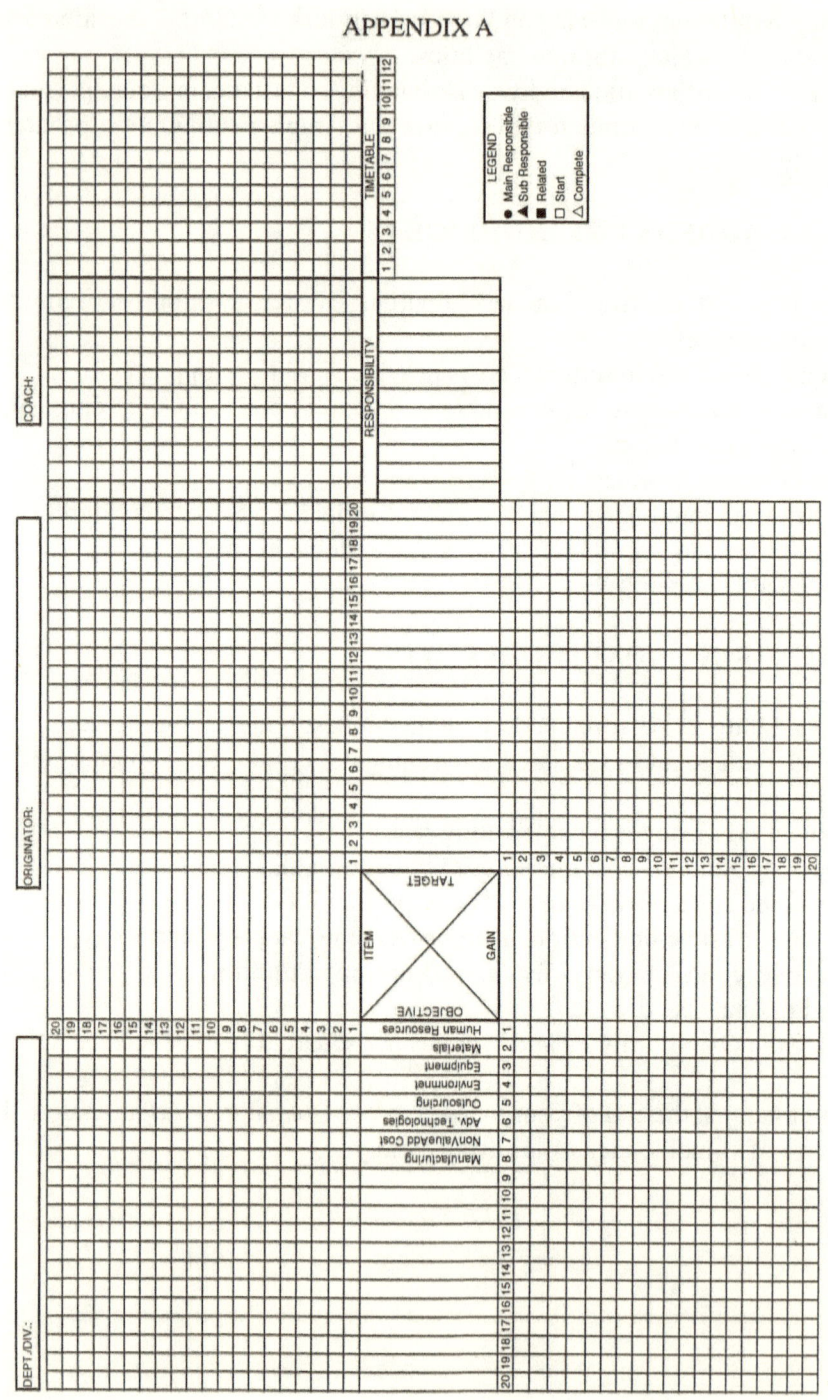

X-Matrix Chart

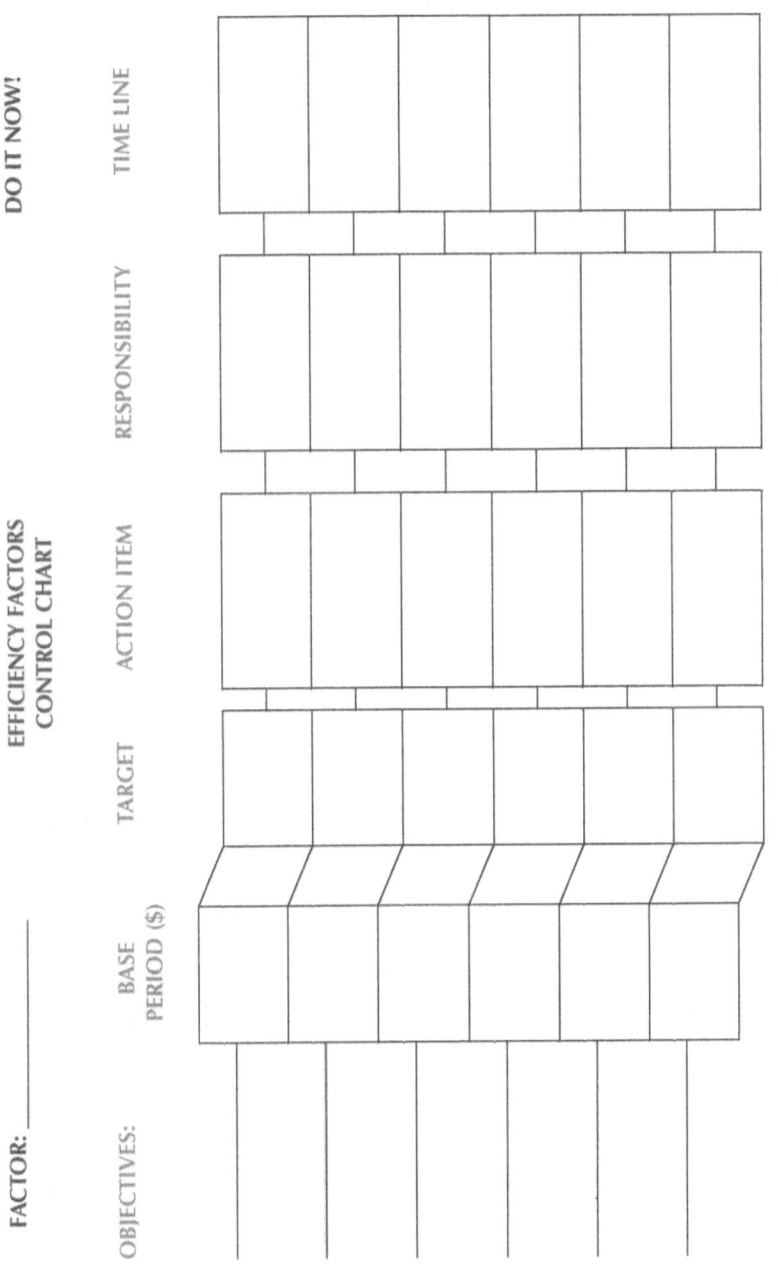

**EFFICIENCY FACTORS
CONTROL CHART**

DO IT NOW!

FACTOR: _____

OBJECTIVES:

BASE PERIOD ($)   TARGET   ACTION ITEM   RESPONSIBILITY   TIME LINE

THE COMPETITIVE EDGE

Joseph J. McHugh

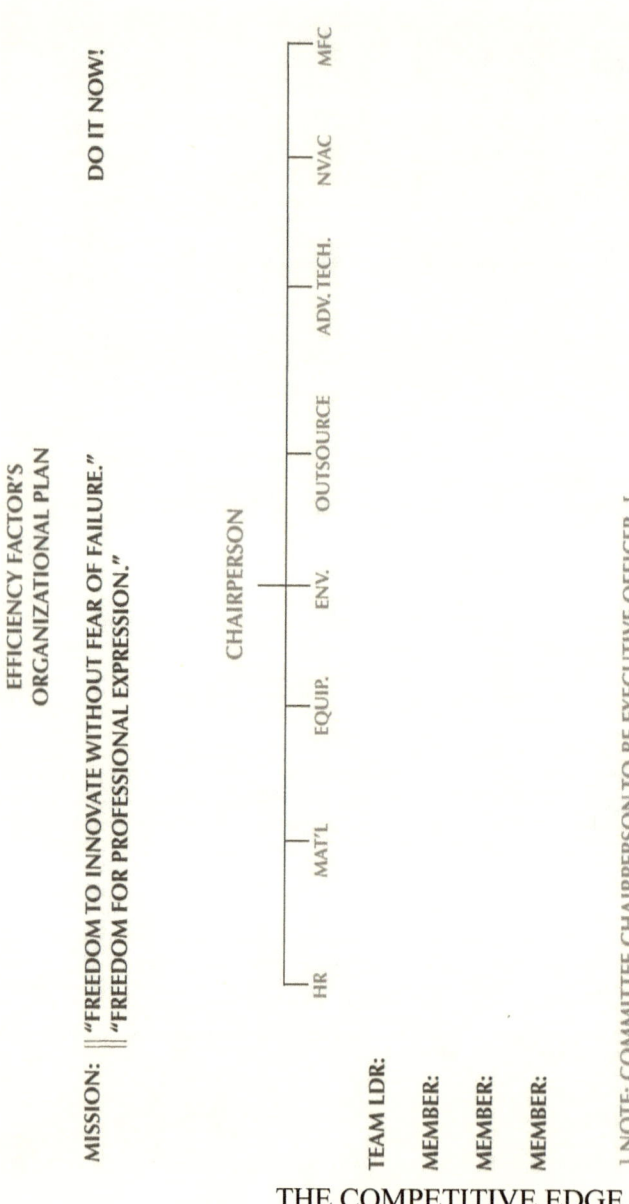

EFFICIENCY FACTOR'S
ORGANIZATIONAL PLAN

MISSION: ‖ "FREEDOM TO INNOVATE WITHOUT FEAR OF FAILURE."
‖ "FREEDOM FOR PROFESSIONAL EXPRESSION."

DO IT NOW!

CHAIRPERSON

HR   MAT'L   EQUIP.   ENV.   OUTSOURCE   ADV. TECH.   NVAC   MFC

TEAM LDR:
MEMBER:
MEMBER:
MEMBER:

] NOTE: COMMITTEE CHAIRPERSON TO BE EXECUTIVE OFFICER. [

THE COMPETITIVE EDGE

Joseph J. McHugh

APPENDIX C

70

About The Author

Mr. McHugh is a seasoned manufacturing executive with 25 years of domestic and international experience (Italy, Poland &, Japan) in consumer electronics. He has assisted in the start-up of facilities, profitable turn-around assignments as well as phase-out of non-competitive businesses. He is a no-nonsense executive with a firm commitment to continuous improvements believing top management does not shutdown businesses or facilities rather local employees and management do because they fail to provide top management with a solid track record of continuous improvements.

His experience further suggests one does not have to completely understand the technology, rather one has to have the drive and determination to move any organization to higher levels of productivity. As Mr. McHugh offers: "Management will no longer accept the inefficiencies of the past nor the passiveness of the present, but rather will be more demanding of the future. The ever expanding global economy demands continual improvements, something Mr. McHugh is committed too.